Caryl
Bryer
Fallert

A Spectrum of Quilts
1983-1995

Booking Information:

For information on booking this
exhibition for other locations,
contact Eric Reid (registrar)
Museum of the American
Quilter's Society, PO Box
1540, Paducah, KY 42002-
1540

Phone 502-442-8856 or
Fax (502-442-5448)

EXHIBITION
TRAVELING SCHEDULE

As of January 1996 a portion of this exhibition
is scheduled to travel to the following locations:

Museum of the American Quilter's Society, Paducah, KY
March 9 – June 15, 1996

Illinois Art Gallery, State of Illinois Building, Chicago, IL
July 12 – Sept. 6, 1996

The Illinois State Museum Gallery, Lockport, IL
September 22 – November 3, 1996

Illinois State Museum, Springfield, IL
Nov. 16, 1996 – Feb. 2, 1997

Dunedin Fine Art Center, Dunedin, FL
June 27– August 15, 1997

New England Quilt Museum, Lowell, MA
Oct. 30, 1997 – January 3, 1998

Caryl Bryer Fallert

A Spectrum of Quilts
1983-1995

American Quilter's Society
P. O. Box 3290 • Paducah, KY 42002-3290

Located in Paducah, Kentucky, the American Quilter's Society (AQS), is dedicated to promoting the accomplishments of today's quilters. Through its publications and events, AQS strives to honor today's quilt-makers and their work — and inspire future creativity and innovation in quiltmaking.

PHOTOS: Caryl Bryer Fallert, unless otherwise noted.

Library of Congress Cataloging-in-Publication Data

Fallert, Caryl Bryer.
    Caryl Bryer Fallert: a spectrum of quilts, 1983 – 1995 / Caryl Bryer
Fallert.
        p. cm.
    Exhibition catalog.
    ISBN 0-89145-874-3
    1. Fallert, Caryl Bryer — Exhibitions. 2. Quilts — United States —
History — 20th century — Exhibitions.
I. Title.
NK9198.F35A4   1996   95-52922
746.46 092–dc20   CIP

Additional copies of this book may be ordered from: American Quilter's Society, P.O. Box 3290, Paducah, KY 42002-3290 @ $24.95. Add $2.00 for postage & handling.

Printed in the U.S.A. by Image Graphics

To my Mother and Father

who encouraged my
sense of wonder
and to

Bob

who continues to support it.

TABLE OF CONTENTS

FOREWORD

When Caryl Bryer Fallert began quilting in 1983, little did the world know what she had in store for it. My own first encounter with a Caryl Fallert quilt was a hand-made piece entitled "Red Poppies," which was submitted to the American Quilter's Society for publication in *Quilt Art '85*. Meredith and I were just beginning to purchase quilts for the quilt museum we planned to build. We immediately purchased "Red Poppies."

Caryl's next quilt that caught my eye was "Morning Glory Trellis." By the time this piece was featured in our popular *Quilt Art* engagement calendar series, Meredith and I were well into the design stages for building the Museum of the American Quilter's Society. Unable to acquire this quilt, we arranged to have its design executed in stained glass for the museum's lobby.

Then Caryl stunned the quilt world as she won the Best of Show award in the 1989 AQS Quilt Show & Contest with her masterpiece "Corona II: Solar Eclipse." This spectacular quilt was the first totally machine-made quilt ever selected by judges for receiving this prestigious award.

The Museum of the American Quilter's Society is very proud to have such an important — and visually stunning — quilt in its permanent collection. It is not unusual to hear visitors exclaim, "There it is!" as "Corona II" enters their view in the exhibit gallery. When "Corona II" is at rest in the storage vault, visitors are disappointed. I once asked Caryl if she could duplicate the quilt so that it could always be hanging. She smiled and simply said, "Surely you jest."

Caryl continues to create extraordinary quilts, ever exploring new territory with her designs and techniques. And her achievements continue to be recognized by contest judges, exhibit curators, and textile collectors alike. In 1995 Caryl became the only two-time winner of the Best of Show award at the annual AQS Quilt Show & Contest when her quilt "Migration #2" was selected by the judges for this coveted honor.

The quilt world is much the richer because of Caryl and her work. Like many, I look forward to enjoying Caryl's work through this publication and the exhibits it will accompany, and, as always, I can hardly wait to see the next piece of fabric art she will create.

Bill Schroeder
Co-Founder of AQS & MAQS

A SPECTRUM OF QUILTS

For as long as I can remember, I have expressed myself through artwork. My formal training was primarily in design, drawing, and studio painting. After many years of painting, sewing, and experimenting with other media, I discovered that fabric, as an artistic medium, best expressed my personal vision. I love the tactile qualities of cloth, and the unlimited color range made possible by hand dyeing and painting.

For the last 14 years, I have been a quiltmaker, that is, my work is constructed from layers of fabric stitched together with batting in between. The focus of my work is on qualities of color, line, and texture that will engage the spirit and emotions of viewers. Illusions of movement, depth, and luminosity are common to most of my work.

Several years ago I was asked, "What are your quilts about?" Most of my quilts are about intangibles — seeing, experiencing, and imagining, rather than pictorial representations of any specific object or species. When recognizable objects appear, they are usually metaphors for feelings or ideas. In the process of examining the subject matter of my quilts, I discovered that without any conscious planning on my part, more than half were about sky, or things that happen in the sky, such as birds, flight, astronomy, etc. I suppose I shouldn't be surprised, since I have spent the last 26 years of my life working in the sky as a flight attendant. Sky, air, flight, and birds have all become my personal symbols for the ultimate feeling of freedom. From the farm where I live in Northern Illinois, I can see vast expanses of sky, and almost every day, flocks of birds, geese, herons, egrets, and others. I often feel that I would like to be one of them flying so unencumbered in the open sky. My flowers are metaphors for the centering and grounding that allow the spirit to rest and renew itself. Spirals symbolize the unfolding and opening up of life. The search for a balance between flight and grounding, unfurling and centering is a recurring theme.

My work is also unapologetically about joy, energy, healing — about things that are positive and life-affirming. When my work grows out of life events that are sad or difficult, I make a conscious choice to use that which engenders hope.

I seldom make a quilt based upon a single image. Like a sponge, I soak up visual impressions from everything around me — in my travels, in my everyday life, in the books I read, and in the media I watch. All of these visual impressions become part of

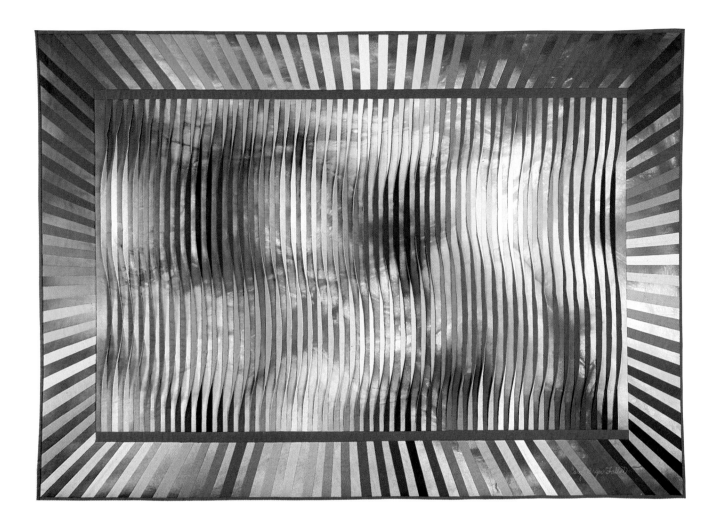

what I like to call my "unconscious visual vocabulary." These images come back to me in my dreams and in my imagination. Sometimes they emerge in ways I don't understand at the time I am using them. It is not unusual for me to finish a design, thinking that it has just popped into my head out of the clear blue, and only after the quilt is finished do I discover the source of the idea.

The most important question I have ever asked myself as an artist is, "What would happen if I ...." I have always had a sense of wonder about the universe and how it works. Fortunately, my curiosity has always been stronger than my fear of failure. Most of my art has grown out of "what would happen if" questions. I get an idea or a vision in my head, and I just have to know how it would look, or if it would work, so I make the quilt. Not all of the "what ifs" have pleased me. Often, however, those scrapped along the way become stepping stones to new discoveries and ultimately to work that *does* please me. While at work on one quilt, my mind is

Reflection #30
60" x 42", 1993

Often a quilt involves several different techniques. The background fabric for this high tech tucks quilt was painted with fiber reactive dyes. The left sides of the tucks were made from pure rainbow hues. The right sides of the tucks graduate from deep blue-violet to white. The three dimensional center of the quilt is finished on the top and bottom by a narrow border of deep purple, followed by a string pieced border of stripes that alternate between the painted background fabric and the colors used in the three dimensional tucks.

frequently exploring how I might make the next one more interesting. Such thinking has led to the development of several series in which one idea leads to the next.

This retrospective exhibition includes examples from several different series of quilts made since 1983, when I began making quilts to hang on the wall. To illustrate how one idea flows from a previous idea, and into the next idea I have organized the quilts into groups — series that have a continuous theme or flow of images, techniques, or ideas. It is important to note, however, that I seldom start a series and make one quilt after another until that series is done. Most of the series are ongoing. I work on them alternately, or concurrently, and often elements of one merge into the next.

My first quilts such as "Red Poppies" and "Cathedral Window" were variations on traditional designs, and could have been used on a bed, although I preferred them on the wall. By 1984 I had begun making quilts that were meant only for the wall. I have used many different techniques in my work. For me, a technique is just a means of expression, a tool, not the expression itself. For each quilt, I try to select the techniques that will best communicate the vision in my head.

String piecing is a technique I have used in one way or another, in almost all of my quilts. To string piece, you first cut a template out of paper or cloth. Then you sew strips of fabric to it, one after another, until it's covered. Next you add a seam allowance, and sew it to the next template. One of the advantages of string piecing is that the strips can vary in width and in the angle at which they are sewn. The templates can be any shape, thus freeing the quiltmaker from the regular grid structure of traditional quilt blocks. In past times when fabric was a precious commodity, every scrap was saved. The long stringy strips that were left over along the selvage after a garment had been cut out of cloth were called "strings"; thus the name for the technique incorporating these narrow, irregular strips into quilts became "string piecing." A number of contemporary quilt artists have reinvented this traditional technique, calling it foundation piecing, paper piecing, etc.

In some quilts (the "Corona" quilts, "Garden Party," "Flying Free #1 & #2," and "Cosmic Pelican"), the entire quilts were string pieced — that is, I made a full-size drawing of the quilt on paper. The drawing was then cut up and strips of fabric were sewn directly to the paper templates. Finally, the entire picture was reassembled like a giant puzzle. In others quilts, string piecing was used in part of the quilt as a means of achieving a particular visual effect. In the tuck quilts, the backgrounds are often string pieced, and even more often the borders are string pieced. Most of my scrap quilts are string pieced, and the triangles that combine to form the illusion quilts are all string

pieced. In quilts like "Migration #2," I have combined areas of string piecing with surface design, machine appliqué, and machine quilting.

My largest group of quilts is my series of three-dimensional tuck quilts. This series began in 1986 after I had been dyeing fabric in gradations of color for two years. I had begun making pleated skirts in which each pleat was a different color in a gradation. One day I wondered, "What would happen if I made a series of tucks with a different gradation of colors on each side?" A couple of experiments led to a series of quilts in which three-dimensional constructed tucks were pieced into a patterned background. The first few had simple, horizontal strip-pieced backgrounds in shades of black, white, and gray. Next I varied the gradations of color that I used and the patterns of the backgrounds. These quilts became a series of experiments in the juxtaposition of color and pattern. By 1990, the tucks had split into at least four sub-series. Checks were added in early 1990 and the "Checking over the Rainbow" group began. By late 1990, I began using fabrics that I had painted with dye as back-

Checking over the Rainbow #7

Side views of this high tech tucks quilt from the left and right, showing the effects of three-dimensional tucks with different colors on each side.

ground. These quilts became the "Reflection" group. In this group, the imagery tends to be more organic. My original "High Tech Tucks" series with geometric pieced backgrounds continued with variations on diagonal lines, intertwining zigzags, and the illusion of transparent, overlapping triangles. The "Aurora" quilts and the "Inner Light" group continue a series about the Aurora Borealis that began in 1985 as two-dimensional string-pieced quilts. Although I do not keep track of how many quilts I have made, I know that the number of tuck quilts is well over 150.

In the "tuck" series, the use of color and value gradations and the twisting of the tucks from side to side create the illusion of movement and light across the surfaces of the quilts. Because different color gradations are used on the right and left sides of the three-dimensional tucks, you can change the appearance of the quilts dramatically by changing your point of view. I like to think of the quilts in this group as "viewer participation art."

The illusion quilts began as a series of experiments for backgrounds in my "High Tech Tucks" series (High Tech Tucks #25–31). Eventually I decided to see how the overlapping triangles would look if I left out the tucks and made them two-dimensional.

In 1984, I began dyeing fabric for my quilts in color and value gradations. In 1989, I began painting fabric, first for clothing, then as backgrounds for "tucks," and finally as fabric for all of my quilts. The quilts I am making presently are made almost exclusively from fabric that I have dyed and painted myself.

My fabric has been painted in every way I can think of, and each time I paint I like to try something new. I have painted with fine sable brushes and sponge rubber brushes. I have sprayed, air brushed, dribbled, and poured dye. Sometimes I even push the dye around with my hands — with gloves of course. The fabric has been smoothed, stretched, folded, scrunched, twisted, pleated, and otherwise manipulated in many different ways. It has been painted wet and painted dry. I have used many techniques that are common to watercolor painting.

In the fall of 1993, I had several of my favorite pieces of painted fabric hanging in my studio. One day I said to myself, "What would happen if I didn't cut these up? What if I just quilted them? People have been known, after all, to make whole-cloth quilts." When I was a painter, it was perfectly fine to paint acrylic or oil pigment onto canvas cloth, then just stretch it and hang it up. "Why must my dye-painted cloth be cut up to become a quilt?" This "what if" question launched a series of whole-cloth quilts. Although several incorporate a small amount of appliqué, the painted surface designs provide the major compositional elements in these quilts tops.

The quilting also becomes a major design element in these pieces, providing a foreground dimension that is contrapuntal to the painted designs. To make the stitches show more clearly, I began using heavy cotton top stitching thread in many different colors for my free-motion machine quilting. Recognizable images in these pieces, such as birds and insects were marked with a fine pencil line. Most of the quilting however, was done freehand, with no marking of the quilt top. I just draw with thread the images that came into my mind — leaves, flowers, spirals, and other organic shapes of undefined origin. This kind of quilting is like doodling with thread. Its patterns are as distinct to the individual quilter as handwriting or a signature.

After a year of making whole-cloth quilts, these began to merge into other groups of quilts. "Migration #2" combines string piecing and appliqué with the whole-cloth technique. Like a number of other quilts, it doesn't clearly fit into any one category.

On the backs of many of my quilts I have included traditional quilt blocks or variations of traditional blocks. Although my quilts are made for the wall and usually don't look "traditional," I feel that my work is part of an on-going tradition. Traditional patchwork motifs are my tribute to the many anonymous quilt artists of the past, who expressed a full range of ideas and emotions in their quilts, even when these quilts were functional, and were not recognized as "art."

So where will I go from here? As I've created this spectrum of quilts, my experience has been that I do my best work when I follow my heart, and don't deliberate too much about it. Lately I have noticed that I am happiest and most content during the *process* of painting, during the *process* of piecing, and during the *process* of machine quilting. The process becomes like meditation, a way of centering my energy. I am learning that to enjoy each color and each stitch is often as important as finishing the quilt.

AWARDS

RED POPPIES

"Red Poppies" is one of a series of medallion quilts I made from 1982 to 1984. Although it is original in design, it conforms to traditional bed-quilt format and has many traditional elements. The center was inspired by my looking through a kaleidoscope. I wanted the quilt to be somewhat floral, so I designed abstract poppies, which are hand appliquéd in each corner of the center panel. The curve of the poppies echoes the curved piecing of the kaleidoscope design.

The outer border was designed to extend and enhance the center. This was the first quilt in which I used curved seams. The entire design was drawn to scale on graph paper and colored in several different color combinations before the piecing began. The outer borders fall into the four patch design category, and the templates for these were made using the paper folding method.

"Red Poppies" was the first quilt I ever entered in a quilt show, and it was the first of my quilts to be published.

AWARDS

Quilters Guild of Dallas 1984
Show: Dallas, TX (First Place)

Silver Dollar City: Spring Arts
and Crafts Festival Show,
1984: Branson, MO (Honor-
able Mention)

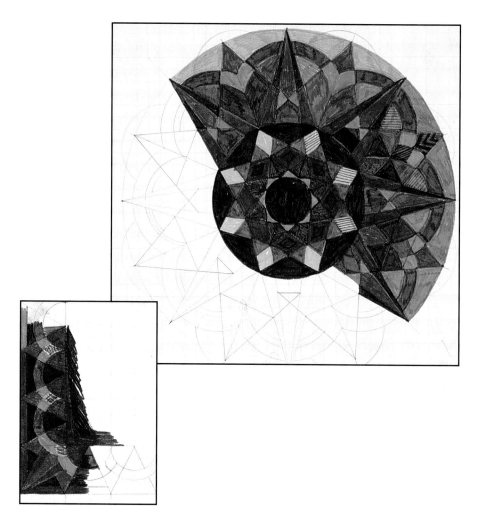

CATHEDRAL WINDOW

The design for this quilt is based on a single central Mariner's Compass. Both the center medallion and the border design were drawn to scale on graph paper before being enlarged to make templates. The spaces between the points of the compass were divided by curved lines.

I wanted to create the feeling of a gothic cathedral window. The fabrics were chosen for their richness and tactile qualities, and include rayon velvet, cotton velveteen, and fabric from men's ties. Because these fabrics are challenging to piece by machine, the entire quilt was pieced and quilted by hand. The back of the quilt is a shiny raspberry satin.

AWARDS

Special Award:
Masterpiece Quilt Award,
National Quilting Association,
1986

Other Awards:
1st Annual AQS Quilt Show &
Contest, 1985, Paducah, KY
(First Place, Other Techniques,
Amateur)

Quilting: New Directions,
1985, Stevens Point, WI (First
Place)

A Quilt Celebration, 1985,
San Jose, CA (First Place &
Best of Show)

Swedish Days Quilt Show,
1985, Geneva, IL (First Place
& Best of Show)

The Vermont Quilt Festival,
1985 (First Place)

National Quilting Association
Show, 1985, Sanford, FL (First
Place, Special Scrap Quilt
Award & Best of Show)

AIQA Quilt Show, 1985,
Houston, TX (Second Place)

Capital City Quilt Festival,
1985, Sacramento, CA (Third
Place)

Silver Dollar City Quilt Show,
1986, Branson, MO (First
Place & Best of Show)

original sketch, 1994

work in progress, 1994

THROUGH THE GAZEBO WINDOW

In this quilt I wanted to create a fabric landscape in the pictorial tradition, with a very literal three-dimensional foreground fading into a more abstract background. My first step was to strip piece 2" strips of over 300 different print and solid fabrics together in sets of three related colors.

The design, a composite of my favorite springtime images, was drawn full size on Bristol board and pinned to the wall of my studio. The garden scene within the window was divided into a series of rhomboid-shaped blocks. Using tracing paper, I traced one block at a time. These tracing paper patterns became the templates for cutting pieces out of my strip-pieced fabric. As each block was pieced, it was pinned to the corresponding section of the drawing. Finally, the blocks were pieced together with bias-cut lattice strips. A single piece of muslin, hand-dyed to look like sky, was used for the back.

The quilt top took three months of intensive work to complete, and the hand quilting took an additional two months.

Urban Maze
102" x 95", 1985
Hand quilted by:
Jeanne Redal, St. Louis, MO

AWARDS

A Holiday Gathering, Eastcoast
Quilters Alliance, 1989, Westford, MA (Third Place)

Rail Fence

URBAN MAZE

This quilt was made from strip-pieced solid and print fabrics left over from "Through the Gazebo Window." My intention was to create the illusion of changes in light, using hundreds of different fabrics.

The arrangement of blocks is loosely based on the traditional Rail Fence pattern. The black sashing was made in graduated sizes and broken up with inserts of color, which give the quilt the look of a maze.

The finished quilt reminded me of an aerial view of a city, hence the title: "Urban Maze." This is the only one of my quilts I have had quilted by another quilter.

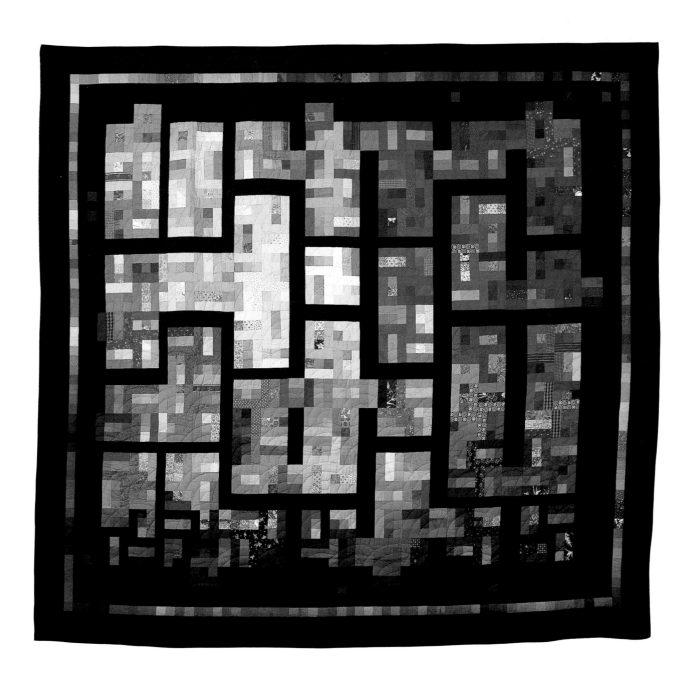

Life in the Margins 2:
After Autumn
52" x 65", 1989

AWARDS

American Quilter's Society
Show, 1989, Paducah, KY
(First Place, Professional Wall
Quilts)

National Quilting Association
Show, 1990, Knoxville, TN
(First Place)

Preliminary doodles for
"Life in the Margins #2:
After Autumn."

"Life in the Margins #2" — back of quilt

LIFE IN THE MARGINS #2: AFTER AUTUMN

At least once each year I make a scrap quilt from leftover strips of fabrics. In 1988, I made a series of quilts in shades of peach and turquoise. This quilt is composed of leftover strips from this series, sewn together in groups of related colors. Equilateral diamonds were cut from the resulting strip-pieced fabric, and these diamonds were pieced together with the lighter values toward the center of the quilt.

The black overlaid design is based on a doodle like those that filled the margins of my school notebooks as a child — thus the title "Life in the Margins." The doodled design was enlarged and machine reverse appliquéd to the pieced background. The machine quilting, which was done freehand with no markings, echoes the doodle design of the black appliqué.

On the back of this quilt is a single large Log Cabin block. I altered it slightly to make it appear to spiral into the center, echoing the spiraling design on the front of the quilt. This variation on a traditional quilt block is my tribute to the creativity of the many anonymous quilt artists of the past.

Refraction #4–#7
Four panels,
43" x 43" each
88" x 88" (in a square)
186" x 43" (in a row)
1990

AWARDS

Quilts=Art=Quilts, Schweinfurth Memorial Arts Center,
1994, Auburn, NY (Judges
Choice)

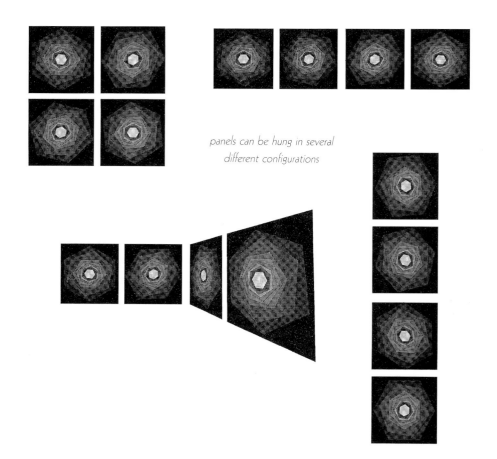

panels can be hung in several
different configurations

REFRACTION #4–#7

"Refraction #4–#7" is composed of four separate panels, which are meant to hang
2"–3" apart. Each panel is slightly different in color and composition, and is meant to
interact visually with the design of the adjacent panel. These panels can be hung in
several different configurations as shown above.

This series of four quilted panels is about luminescence, or light emerging from dark.
"Refraction" refers to the bending of light as it passes through a prism, a crystal, or a
group of raindrops. As a result of refraction, we are able to see the various wave-
lengths of light as a series of individual colors, called a spectrum or simply a rainbow.
The spiraling movement of the pieced design was inspired by pictures of galaxies,
spinning into the dark void of outer space.

The fabrics for this quilt were specially dyed in both chromatic (color to color) and
value (light to dark) gradations to create the illusion of luminescence. The construction
of the panels is based on the traditional Log Cabin piecing technique; however, each
panel is constructed around a hexagon rather than a square. The angling of each suc-
cessive strip of fabric results in the illusion of the bending or spiraling of the light areas.

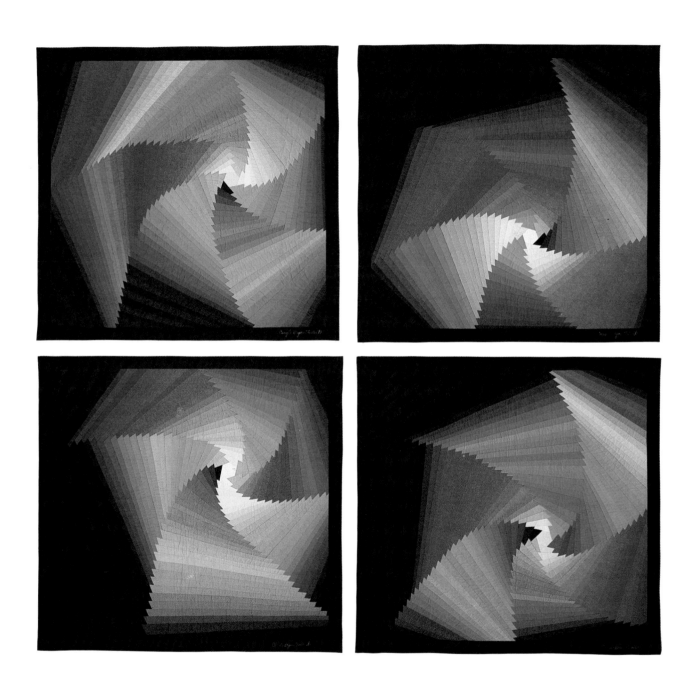

Under the Storm
98" x 98", 1991
Collection of:
Ray & Susan Scott
On permanent loan to:
Museum of the American
Quilter's Society, Paducah, KY

AWARDS

22nd Annual National Quilting
Association Show, 1991, Lincoln, NE (First Place)

UNDER THE STORM

This quilt was based on the traditional Storm at Sea block. Each individual block is 25" square and an 8" border surrounds the nine center blocks. The entire quilt was string pieced. A template for each piece was cut from paper, and strips of fabric in different shades of the same color were sewn to the paper until it was covered. The paper was removed after all of the blocks were assembled.

When I finish a quilt, I toss all my leftover strips of fabric into a laundry basket. By the end of the year, the basket is overflowing with hundreds of colors and shades. With the exception of the 2" outside border, this quilt was made entirely from my 1989 leftovers. Before I began piecing, I sorted strips by color, and then subdivided the colors into light, medium, and dark values. The back of the quilt was pieced from many different blue and green flower prints.

To carry out the Storm at Sea theme, the quilting was done in fish and water patterns. Schools of fantasy fish swim from the upper right corner to the lower left corner of the quilt. Since I wanted the fish to show, I chose a medium gray thread for my machine quilting. It looks dark against the light fabrics and light against the dark fabrics. The spaces between the fish are filled with water patterns quilted freehand.

I chose the name "Under the Storm" when I decided to quilt in fish patterns. I thought that even if there were a storm on the surface of the sea, the fish probably wouldn't care, and would swim peacefully under the surface. Ironically, the day I began quilting the fish was the first day of Operation Desert Storm in the Persian Gulf War. The quilting of the fish became my way of finding peace, during a week when the television news carried around-the-clock reports of frightening events.

Illusion #2
89" x 88", 1993

AWARDS

American Quilter's Society Show, 1993, Paducah, KY (First Place)

Quilt America, 1993, Indianapolis, IN (Third Place)

Speaking of Values, A Quilters Gathering, Eastcoast Quilters, 1994, Westford, MA (First Place – Craftsmanship)

Quilters Unlimited Showcase, 1995, Kansas City, MO (Third Place)

ILLUSION #2

This is one of a series of quilts exploring the illusion of overlapping transparent triangles. The triangles were pieced from strips of fabric hand dyed in value (light to dark) gradations of the three primary colors (turquoise, yellow, fuchsia) and the three secondary colors (green, orange, purple). Each triangle was pieced separately and then cut into horizontal strips. The strips of the two triangles were alternated when they were sewn back together. This creates the illusion of more than one triangle occupying the same space. As the groups of triangles were sewn together, the illusion of long vertical diamonds appeared in the background.

In contrast to the geometry of the pieced design, the quilting was done in a free-form swirling design using shiny rayon embroidery thread in many colors. All of the machine quilting was done freehand, with no marking of the quilt top.

The original design for this quilt was drawn, using Corel Draw!®, a computer assisted design program.

ILLUSION #13

This is another of a series of quilts exploring the illusion of overlapping transparent triangles. Although the visual image is complex, the construction of this quilt was quite simple. The triangles were pieced on a paper foundation using strips of fabric hand dyed in various gradations of light to dark colors. Each triangle was pieced separately and then cut into horizontal strips. The strips of the two triangles were alternated when they were sewn back together to create the illusion of more than one triangle occupying the same space.

A narrow border of black surrounds the center triangles, followed by a wider border of dye-painted fabric. A binding of solid black completes the composition.

The quilting was done in free-form, swirling patterns using variegated cotton thread in rainbow colors. All of the machine quilting was done freehand, with no marking of the quilt top.

CORONA I: SOLAR ECLIPSE

From the time I heard about the first space rockets and satellites as a very young child, I have been fascinated by the solar system and things that happen in the sky. This quilt portrays a solar eclipse, when the disk of the moon comes between the earth and the sun. The corona is the luminous envelope of ionized gasses surrounding the chromasphere of the sun, which is visible during a total solar eclipse.

The quilt is constructed from 100% cotton fabrics, dyed in both chromatic and value gradations. These gradations create the illusion of the fading of the fire of the corona into the gray-mauve of the sky. The entire quilt was string pieced on a paper base. The quilting was done by machine, in a spiraling pattern, radiating out from the side of the moon to the edges of the sky. On the back of the quilt is a single traditional Log Cabin block, pieced in the colors of the quilt top.

This quilt was commissioned in 1987 for the living room of a new home in St. Louis, Missouri. In 1994 the owners sold their home and moved to a condominium with little wall space. I was able to buy the quilt back and it was subsequently purchased by Fairfield Processing Corp. for their permanent collection.

drawing the full size pattern on a piece of paper, 76" x 94"

CORONA II: SOLAR ECLIPSE

This is my second quilt portraying the solar eclipse. I have always been fascinated by the dramatic storms on the surface of the sun, which can flair out into the sky for hundreds of miles. The few minutes during a solar eclipse are the time when astronomers are actually able to observe the solar storms in the corona of the sun. "Corona II: Solar Eclipse" is more a portrayal of my feelings about the power of the sun than an exact representation of what a scientist might see.

The quilt is constructed from 100% cotton fabric, dyed and over-dyed in both chromatic and value gradations. These gradations create the illusion of fire and swirling motion on the surface of the quilt. Both the front and back of the quilt are string pieced. I chose Robbing Peter to Pay Paul as my traditional block for this quilt, because it is based on a circle and carries out the circular theme of the sun and moon on the front of the quilt.

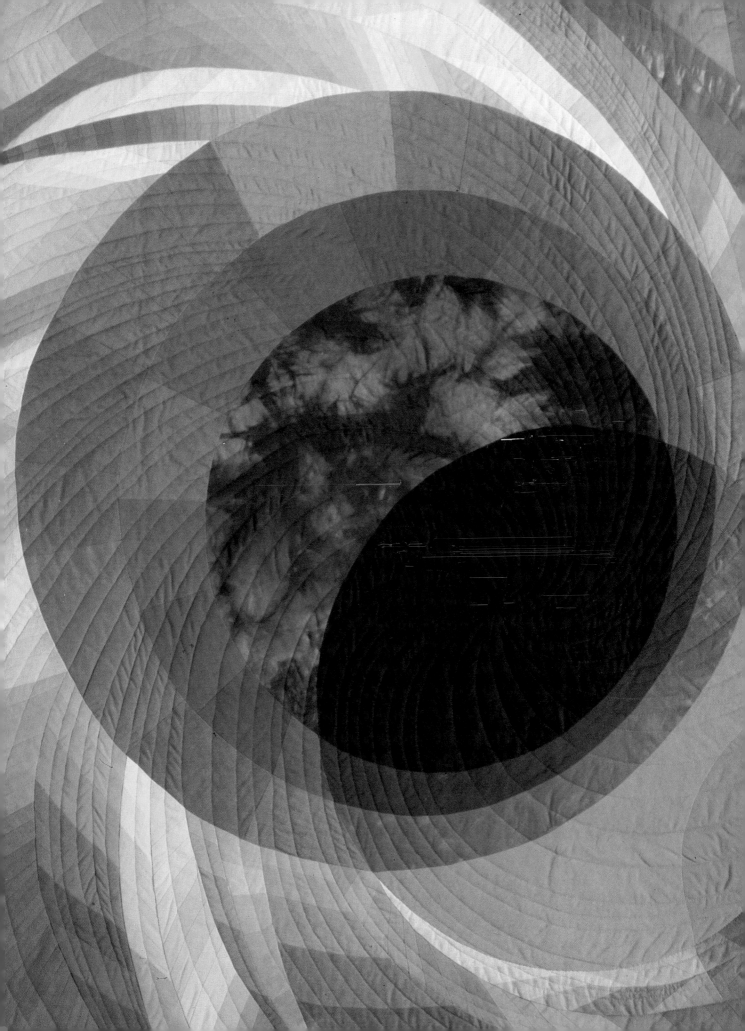

"Corona II: Solar Eclipse," back

Garden Party
49" x 61", 1989
Collection of:
Ray & Susan Scott

AWARDS

American International Quilt
Association Show, 1989,
Houston, TX (First Place)

work in progress, 1989

GARDEN PARTY

The design for this quilt was based on a series of thumbnail sketches and color render-
ings done over a two year period from 1987 to 1989. The sketches began with
organic shapes derived from nature. The design was developed by repeating these
shapes at various angles, and doodling in connecting lines. A full-size drawing was
done, based on the sketches, but not an exact copy of any one of them. The full-size
drawing was cut up, and each individual section was used as a template for string
piecing. The pieces of the picture were then reassembled using a construction method
that is a cross between appliqué and piecing.

The theme of this quilt is the sense of wonder, mystery, beauty, and serenity to be
found on a visit to an exotic tropical garden. The shapes do not represent any particular botanical species.

The machine quilting was done freehand, with no marking. The back of the quilt is a
single large Log Cabin block made from the strips of fabric left over from the front.

Cosmic Pelican
58" x 68", 1992
Collection of:
Ray & Susan Scott

AWARDS

Mid-Atlantic Quilt Festival, 1993, Williamsburg, VA (Second Place)

American Quilter's Society Show, 1993, Paducah, KY (Third Place, Pictorial Wall Quilt)

COSMIC PELICAN

The design for this quilt began in 1990 with a simple line drawing of a pelican grooming itself. It was put in a drawer full of miscellaneous sketches for two years. Every time I opened that drawer, the pelican seemed to beckon to me. Several times in 1991, I got the drawing out and played with the design, changing it and expanding it in different ways. When it was time to make the quilt in 1992, the final sketch was translated into a full-size drawing.

Since the theme of the quilt is more about letting the imagination fly than it is about the pelican as a species of bird, I chose fantasy colors. The bird is pieced from fabric dyed in various gradations of blue, green, and turquoise, and he is surrounded by ribbons of rainbow colors and a swirling warm-toned background. He really became a silly fellow who, although he is only a pelican, seems to think he is a cross between a phoenix and a peacock.

The inner borders of the quilt are striped and hand woven ikat fabric. The 8" outer border was string pieced from the graduated warm hues used in the background, broken occasionally by rainbow colors. The machine quilting was done freehand, with no marking.

On the back of the quilt is a variation of the traditional Flying Geese pattern.

AWARDS

American International Quilt
Association Show, Quilt Festival,
1994, Houston, TX (First
Place)

"Crabby" Award for Excellence
in the Visual Arts, 1995, *Art
Calendar Magazine*

Quilt America, 1995, Kokomo,
IN (Third Place)

FLYING FREE #1

This quilt was made in fall 1993, at a time when I was physically exhausted. I had flown full time for the airline for the entire summer, and in May through September had also flown over 25,000 miles as a passenger, to teach in locations like New Zealand, Fairbanks, and Honolulu. One September morning I awoke with an idea for a new quilt. I must have dreamed it. I don't often have ideas that just pop into my head, so I've learned to pay attention to them. I ran out to my studio at seven in the morning and did a series of small sketches, trying to capture the idea before it escaped. The title was in my head too: "Flying Free." For me flight has always symbolized the ultimate freedom. I wanted to capture that essence in my design. I felt compelled to work on the quilt even though I was leaving for Switzerland within a few days. I chose the thumbnail sketch I liked the best, and put it through a series of evolutions and mutations until I had a final design. This was projected onto paper to make a full-size drawing. The quilt has several layers of visual activity, all weaving in and out of each other. As I was piecing the quilt I began to understand my dream.

After 25 years as a flight attendant, I was ready to stop flying, even though I had three and a half years left before I could retire. I imagined that not having to get on a plane any more would give me the ultimate feeling of freedom that flying symbolized for me. Ironically, what was preventing me from having that ultimate freedom was, in fact, flying.

A variation of the traditional Flying Geese quilt block is incorporated into one of the curved and tapered templates. The free-form machine quilting was done with clear nylon filament.

Caryl Bryer Fallert

Flying Free #2
82" x 93", 1995

AWARDS

Quilt America, 1995, Kokomo, IN (Honorable Mention)

From Patches to Neon, Pennsylvania National Quilt Extravaganza II, 1995, Fort Washington, PA (Best of Show)

American International Quilt Association Show, 1995, Houston, TX (Award of Excellence)

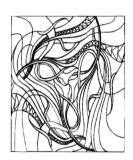

FLYING FREE #2

This is one of a series of quilts exploring the idea of flights of the imagination. From my farm in northern Illinois, I can see vast expanses of sky and huge flocks of migrating geese. My more immediate surroundings are filled with the vines, leaves, flowers, and vegetables in my garden. All of these images have found their way into the abstract design of this quilt, and each image is inseparably intertwined or interconnected with the next, as they are in life.

The design was created in winter 1994, using a computer program to manipulate the hand drawn design I had used previously for "Flying Free #1." When the design was complete, it was drawn onto a piece of paper the size of the finished quilt with the assistance of an overhead projector. The piecing of "Flying Free #2" began in early April 1995, and the quilt was finished in early June.

A variation of the traditional Flying Geese block is incorporated into three of the curved and tapered templates. The freehand, free motion machine quilting contains many organic images of leaves and flowers. Heavy (#30) cotton top stitching thread in many different colors was used so the quilting patterns would show up clearly against the fabric of the quilt top. Matching threads were used in the bobbin and can be clearly seen on the quilt back.

A single graduated line of Flying Geese curves and loops diagonally across the back of the quilt, fading gradually into the background of dark painted fabric as it nears the upper right corner. This quilt is dedicated to the memory of my mother, whose spirit was set free the week it was completed.

"Flying Free #2," back

ME AND MY 404 BLUES

This quilt was originally designed for a show called "A Palette of Prisms" in Cazenovia, NY. The design limitation set by the show was to work in twelve shades of a single color. The color I chose for my hand-dyed fabric was blue #404 from Pro Chemical and Dye Co. A silkscreen was made from a photograph of me sitting at my sewing machine working on one of my three-dimensional tuck quilts. The dark blue "weed cloth" fabric began as dark blue hand-dyed fabric, which was discharged with chlorine bleach. The pattern was created by real willow leaves from a tree in my front yard.

In this quilt I experimented with combining modules of three-dimensional tucks and two-dimensional patchwork. The overall design is based on a traditional Eight-Pointed Star. By enlarging the star, and then further dividing the spaces within the star, the design became a complex medallion.

The back of this quilt is pieced in a series of traditional Ohio Star blocks.

AWARDS

American Quilter's Society
Show 1988, Paducah, KY
(First Place, Innovative Pieced,
Professional)

American International Quilt
Association Show, 1989,
Houston, TX (First Place)

CHROMATIC PROGRESSIONS: AUTUMN

This is one of only two quilts in which I have combined curved string piecing with three-dimensional constructed tucks. Cotton fabric dyed in muted gradations of rainbow colors was used to construct the tucks. A different gradation of color was used on each side of the tucks and a third color gradation was used in the background of the interlacing arcs and the outside border. The brown and muted color gradations suggest the feeling of a crisp, sunny, autumn day.

The traditional quilt block Dove in the Window is pieced into the back of this quilt.

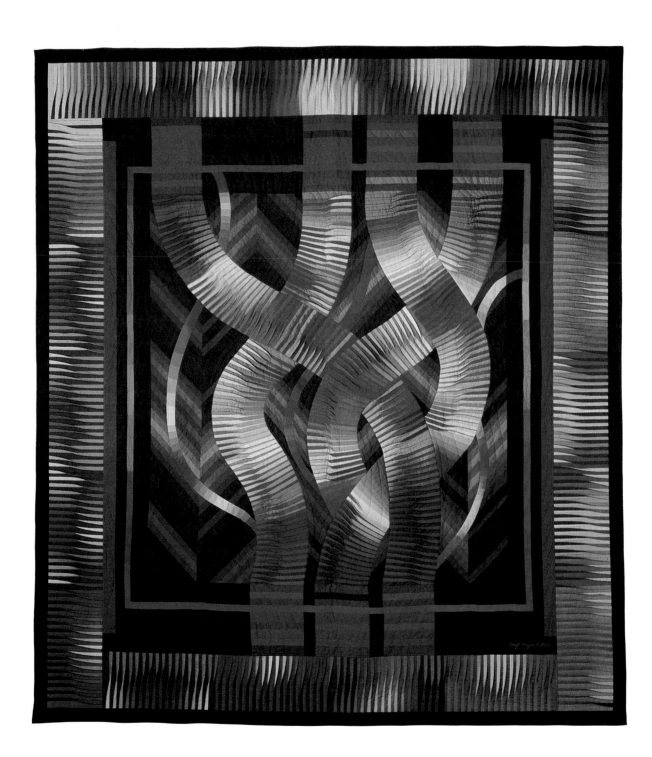

HIGH TECH TUCKS #14

This is one of a series of quilts in which three-dimensional, constructed tucks are incorporated into a pieced background. The fabrics used to piece the background were hand dyed in light to dark gradations of rust and turquoise, as well as gradations that cross between the two colors. The background was string pieced, then cut into strips and reassembled with a tuck in each seam.

Each of the half-inch tucks was constructed from two different fabrics. A different gradation of color and value is used on each side of the tuck. The gradations and the twisting of the tucks from side to side create the illusion of movement and light across the surface of the quilt.

A radiating, string-pieced border continues the visual motion of the center panel of the quilt. It is constructed from alternating strips of fabric, dyed in two different color and value gradations.

A traditional quilt block is pieced into the back of this quilt using fabrics left over from the front.

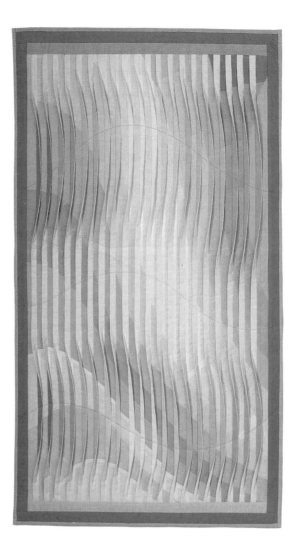
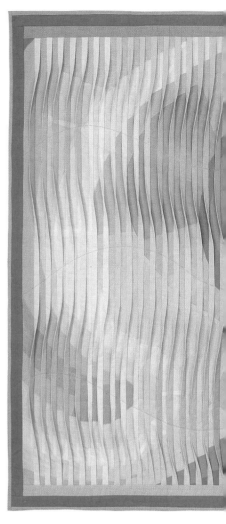

BLIZZARD

This quilt is a visual interpretation of winter snows on the flat open prairies of northern Illinois. It was inspired by the "Great Blizzard of '79," when the snow drifts were not only over my head, but also over the tops of some of the buildings on our farm. After the blizzard, the temperature dropped to well below zero, and the snow became granulated. For weeks after the storm, this granulated snow swirled into drifts and dunes in the open fields. When the sun came out all the shadows were turquoise.

The background was pieced in a single swirling design using fabric dyed in shades of blue and turquoise. One side of the tucks are a gradation of blue and the other a gradation of turquoise. On the back of the center panel is a large Grandmother's Flower Garden block. I chose a hexagonal design to echo the geometric structure of snowflakes.

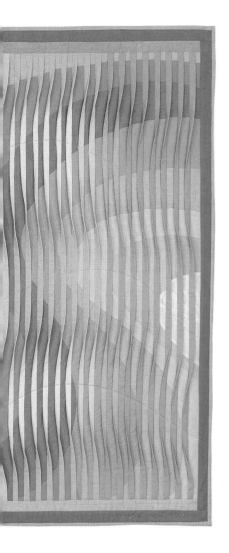

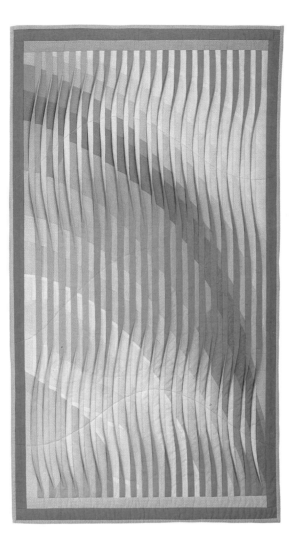

snow drifts on the farm, "Great Blizzard of '79"

CHECKING OVER THE RAINBOW #8

This is the eighth in a sub-series of tuck quilts exploring various relationships between checks and gradations of rainbow colors. The background strips alternate between black and white 1" checks and black 1" checks arranged against a gradation of rainbow colors.

The left sides of the tucks are a gradation of pure rainbow colors. The right sides of the tucks graduate from black to white, with black and white checks in the center.

The center of the quilt is framed by a narrow border of black and white checks, followed by a wider string-pieced border and a binding of black and white checks. The strips of the radiating string-pieced border alternate between checks against rainbow colors and shades of solid black, gray, and white.

On the back of this quilt is a Courthouse Steps variation of the traditional Log Cabin quilt block.

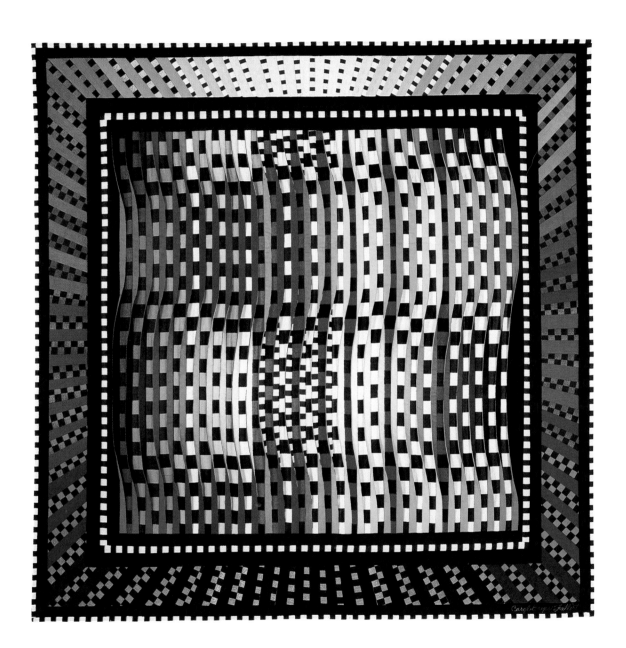

Inner Light #4
71" x 49", 1993

AWARDS

Quilt Connection All Stars,
Great American Quilt Festival,
Museum of American Folk Art,
1993, New York, NY, and
traveling (Honorable Mention)

American International Quilt
Association Show, 1994:
Houston, TX (Award of Merit)

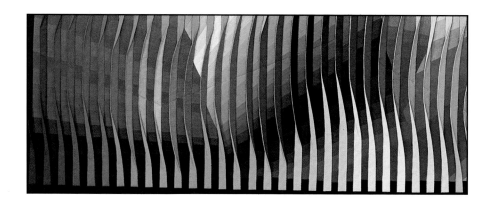

INNER LIGHT #4

The background for "Inner Light #4" was string pieced from fabric dyed in a spectrum of pure rainbow colors, as well as pure colors gradually fading to black. The divisions of space in the background are unevenly spaced diagonal and triangular areas. While there are areas of contrast occurring along the seams of the diagonal areas, overall the contrast is subtle and appears to emerge and fade along any given line.

Each of the 59 tucks is constructed from two different fabrics. The right sides of the tucks are made from fabrics dyed in a gradation of pure hues, which include the entire spectrum of colors. The left sides of the tucks are gradations from the three primary colors (turquoise, yellow, fuchsia) and the three secondary colors (orange, purple, green) to black. Color and value gradations create the illusion of light emerging from within the quilt, and the twisting of the tucks from side to side creates the illusion of movement across the surface of the quilt. Inner light has been a recurring theme in many of my quilts during the last five years. It interests me both as a symbol of enlightenment and as a purely visual phenomenon.

A radiating, string-pieced border surrounds the three-dimensional center panel. All colors of the spectrum are used in the border. Strips of these colors alternate with strips of black in the bottom and side borders. In the top border strips of rainbow hues alternate with strips dyed in a light to dark gradation of blue-violet.

This is the first quilt I ever designed using a computer assisted drawing program. The background, tucks, and border were each drawn separately and then layered over one another on the computer screen.

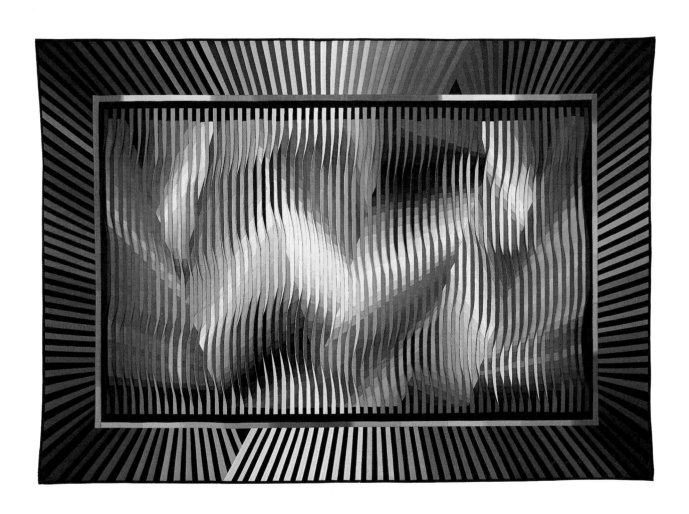

Reflection #1
40" x 36", 1990

REFLECTION #1

This is the beginning of a series of quilts in which constructed tucks are incorporated into a background of painted fabric. The background fabric was painted with fiber reactive dyes in a design that suggests water flowers. These flower forms represent the flowering of the imagination rather than any particular botanical species.

The left sides of the tucks were made from fabrics dyed in a gradation of warm hues, from purple to red to yellow. The right sides of the tucks were dyed in a gradation of cool colors from purple to blue to green. The use of color gradations and the twisting of the tucks from side to side create the illusion of movement and light across the surface of the quilt.

The radiating string-pieced border is constructed from alternating strips of painted fabric and the color gradations used to make the tucks.

Reflection #3
45" x 77", 1990
Collection of:
Museum of the American
Quilter's Society,
Paducah, KY

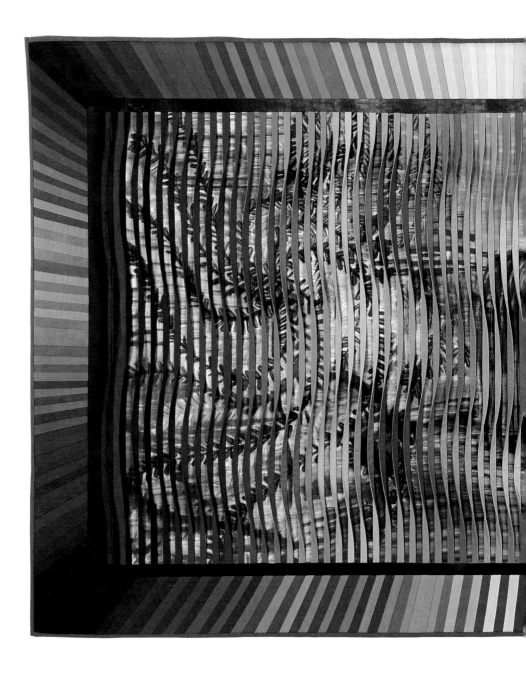

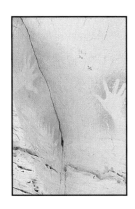

aboriginal rock paintings

REFLECTION #3

The background fabric for "Reflection #3" portrays my memory of Carnarvon Gorge National Park, a beautiful, peaceful place we visited in Australia in 1989. This dramatic gorge is filled with exotic vegetation, some of it prehistoric and found in very few places on earth. In a number of locations throughout the gorge are found 10,000-year-old aboriginal rock paintings in the red and yellow ocher colors of the soil. After a long, hot day of hiking, we climbed into a side canyon called the "Moss

Carnarvon Gorge National Park, Australia

Garden" and found a cool, green peaceful place where both the spirit and the body could rest. This quilt is about the entire experience. The patterns in the background fabric represent the foliage, rocks, streams, and waterfalls of the gorge. The fabrics for the left sides of the tucks were dyed in gradations of the greens, blues, and mauves of the exotic foliage. The right sides of the tucks are the red and yellow ocher colors of the aboriginal rock paintings.

REFLECTION #17

The background fabric for "Reflection #17" was stretched on a large wooden frame and painted with fiber reactive dyes in a radiating design of pure, intense, rainbow hues. The right sides of the tucks were made from fabrics dyed in a gradation of values from white to navy blue to black. The left sides of the tucks are a 44 hue gradation of pure rainbow colors. Lattice strips between the horizontal sections of tucks are made from hand-painted, rainbow striped fabric.

The radiating, string-pieced border is constructed from alternating strips of solid gradu-ated colors and hand-painted striped fabric.

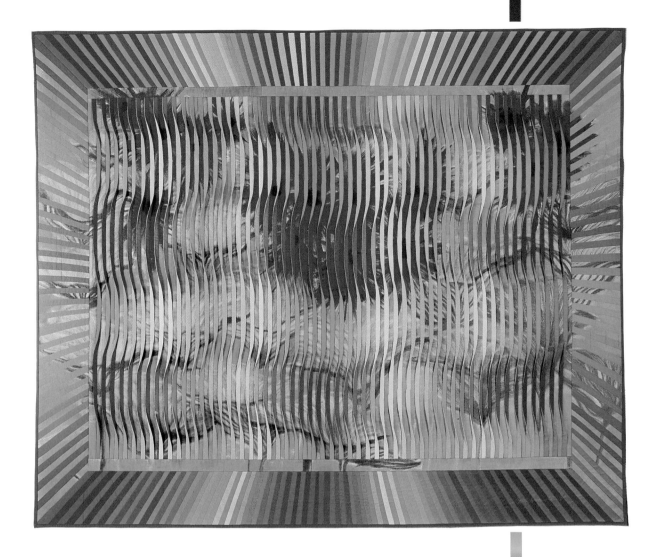

REFLECTION #18

The background fabric for "Reflection #18" was painted with fiber reactive dyes in large flower and leaf patterns. These patterns represent the feeling of floating among water flowers and seeing them at very close range. The right sides of the tucks were made from fabrics dyed in a gradation of pure rainbow hues. The left sides of the tucks were dyed in a value gradation of turquoise.

The radiating, string-pieced border extends the background of flower and leaf patterns, while drawing the eye back into the center panel.

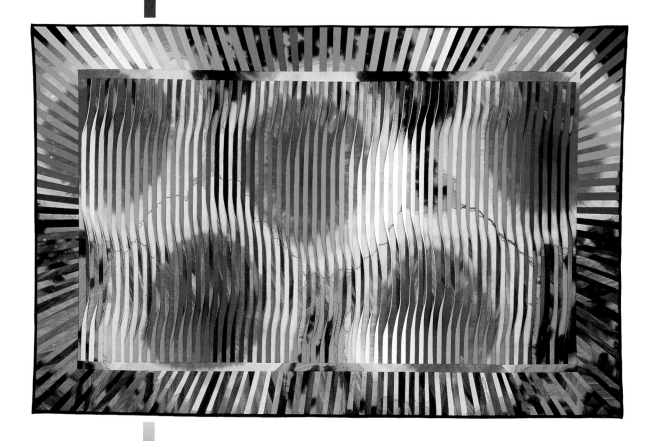

Reflection #19
63" x 40", 1991

REFLECTION #19

The background fabric for "Reflection #19" was stretched on a large wooden frame and painted with dye in large flower and leaf patterns. The abstract flower forms are like sunbursts of pure color. These patterns represent the feeling of looking straight down into the center of flowers.

The right sides of the tucks were made from fabrics dyed in a gradation of values from white to turquoise to black. The left sides of the tucks are a fabric that was painted in shades of green to represent grass and leaves. A radiating, string-pieced border extends the background of yellow flower forms, while drawing the eye back into the center panel.

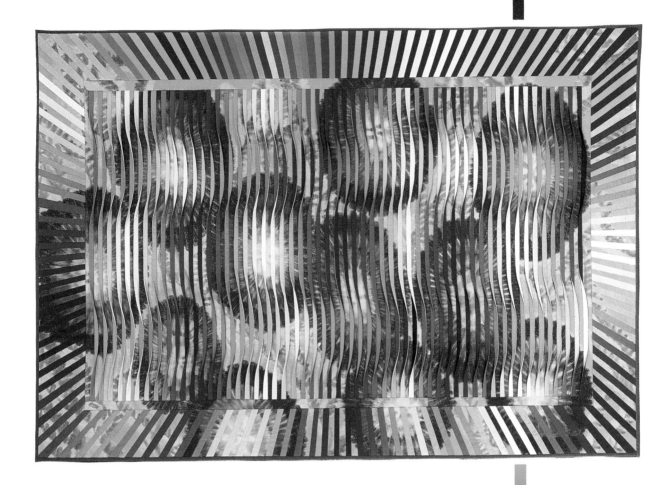

REFLECTION #21

Reflection #21
63" x 51", 1991

The flower and leaf patterns of the painted background fabric were inspired by English asters in full bloom just outside my dye studio. They are the last flowers to bloom before the frost kills everything in the fall. They have escaped from the flower bed and grow like weeds everywhere. My husband has engaged them in battle. I'm rooting for the asters.

The right sides of the tucks were made from fabrics dyed in a light to dark gradation of blue-violet. The left sides of the tucks are light to dark gradations of both green and turquoise. A radiating string-pieced border extends the background of purple flower forms and repeats the solid colors used in the tucks.

AWARDS

American International Quilt Association Show, 1992, Houston, TX (Award of Merit)

Protecting and Replenishing Our Earth's Resources, Chesapeake Quilt Festival, 1993, Townson, MD (Second Place)

Quilts=Art=Quilts, Schweinfurth Memorial Art Center, 1993–94, Auburn, NY (First Place)

REFLECTION #27

The background fabric was spray painted with fiber reactive dyes using real leaves to create a pattern of leaves in rainbow hues floating on a dark ground. The leaves were weeds growing in my flower beds. The left sides of the tucks were made from fabrics dyed in a 27-color gradation of pure rainbow hues. The right sides of the tucks graduate from the three primary and secondary colors (fuchsia, turquoise, yellow, orange, green, purple) to black.

The center of the quilt is divided into three horizontal panels which are surrounded by a narrow, inner border of small black and rainbow colored stripes. A radiating, string-pieced outer border is constructed from alternating strips of rainbow colors and the color-to-black gradations used to make the tucks.

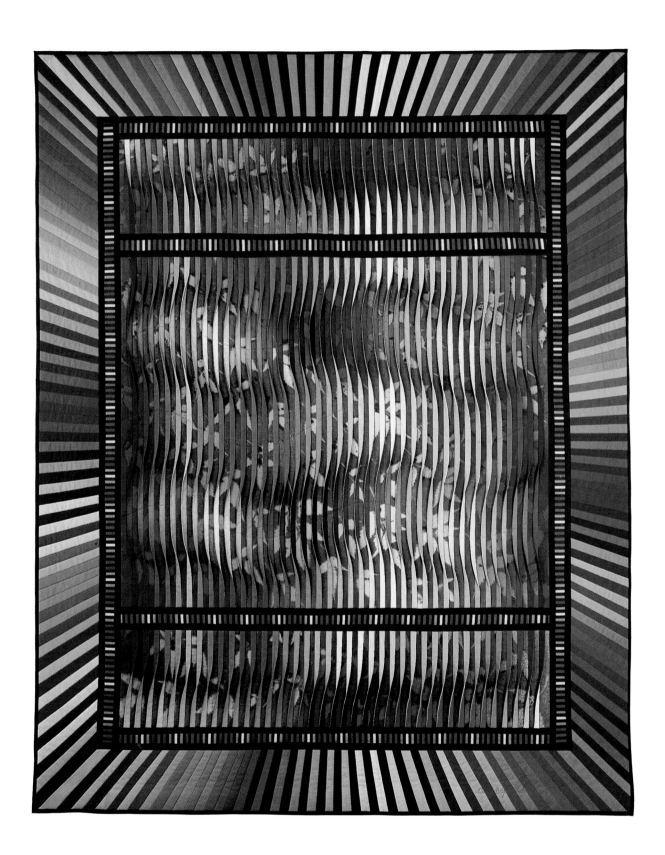

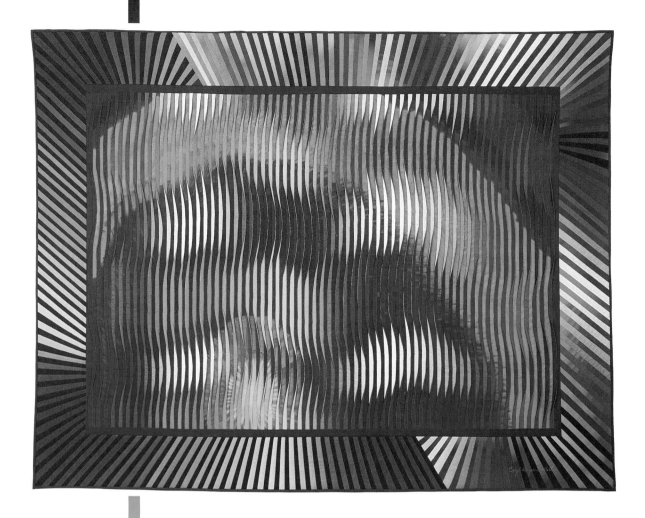

REFLECTION #28

The background fabric for "Reflection #28" was stretched and painted with dye in a radiating design of graduated rainbow hues spinning out from a hot, yellow-orange core, like a surreal sunrise.

The right sides of the tucks are made from fabrics dyed in a 47-color gradation of pure rainbow hues. The left sides of the tucks graduate from black to deep blue-violet to white. Half of the radiating string-pieced border was constructed from alternating strips of rainbow colors and black. In the other half of the border, strips of painted fabric alternate with strips dyed in the black to blue-violet to white gradation used on the left sides of the tucks.

REFLECTION #29

The background fabric for "Reflection #29" was painted with fiber reactive dyes in an expressionistic, free-form design. The left sides of the tucks were made from fabrics dyed in a gradation of colors from yellow-green to plum. The right sides of the tucks graduate from blue-violet to peach. The three-dimensional center of the quilt is surrounded by a narrow border of deep purple, followed by a wider border of the same dye-painted fabric used as background for the tucks.

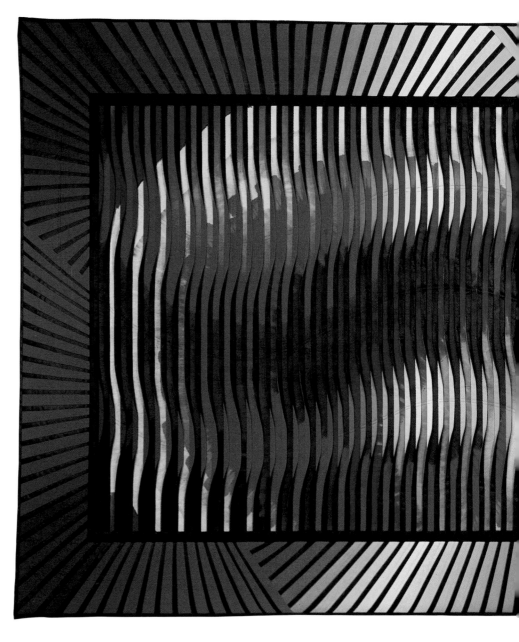

REFLECTION #34

In this quilt, two different background fabrics were used. The first (fabric A) was painted with fiber reactive dyes in a single large sunburst type pattern, beginning with cobalt blue in the center and graduating through purple, fuchsia, and orange, to yellow. The second (fabric B) was painted with two sunburst forms, both beginning with yellow in the center and graduating to purple. The upper right sunburst graduates through all of the colors on the cool side of the color wheel (green, turquoise, blue) and the lower right sunburst graduates through all of the colors on the warm side of the color wheel (orange, red, fuchsia). Both fabrics were cut into 1" wide

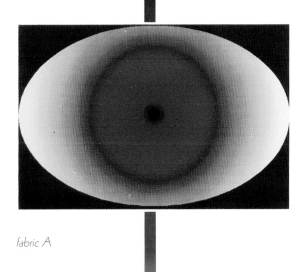

fabric A

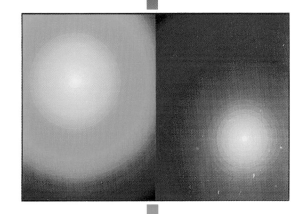

fabric B

strips and sewn back together in alternating strips (A-B-A-B) with a tuck in each seam allowance.

The right sides of the tucks were made from fabrics dyed in a very intense, 46-hue gradation of rainbow colors. The left sides of the tucks were made from black polished cotton. A radiating, string-pieced border surrounds the three-dimensional center panel. The border strips alternate between very narrow strips of black polished cotton and wider strips of the rainbow colors used in the tucks. The outer binding is black polished cotton.

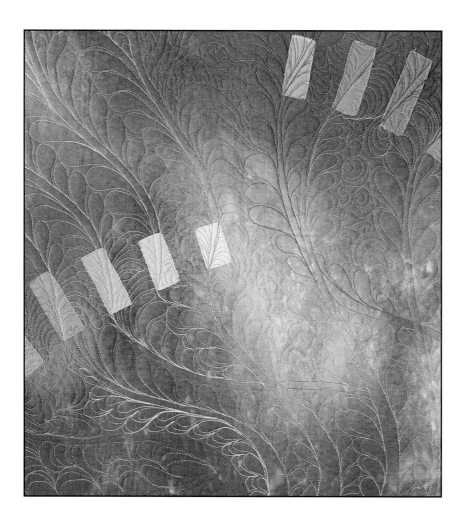

AFTER THE RAIN

This is the first in a series of painted, whole-cloth quilts. The fabric was painted with fiber reactive dye in an expressionistic design. Small bits of fabric dyed in color gradations were laid on the surface and stitched down. The fabric was then layered and quilted heavily by machine in a free-form pattern that was stitched freehand with no marking of the quilt top. The multicolored machine quilting becomes a major design element in this piece, providing a foreground dimension that is contrapuntal to the painted design.

This quilt was begun on the last day of a midwestern summer in which there were only eight sunny days and record flooding in many areas. It represents my delight in the sun, when it finally emerged, and the lush growth of all forms of vegetation, a result of the daily rainfall.

New Growth
58" x 45", 1994

NEW GROWTH

This is the third in a series of dye-painted quilts. A few small bits of fabric dyed in color gradations were cut into circles and leaf shapes and machine appliquéd on the surface. The fabric was then layered and quilted heavily by machine in various organic patterns, which were stitched freehand and incorporated the appliquéd shapes. The machine quilting becomes a major design element in this piece, providing a foreground dimension that is contrapuntal to the painted design.

This quilt was made in the early spring of 1994, following a particularly long and bitterly cold winter. It reflects my feeling of delight at the unfolding and emerging of the natural world at that time of the year.

AWARDS

From Sea to Shining Sea,
(juried), Pennsylvania National
Quilt Extravaganza, Philadelphia,
PA (Honorable Mention)

Quilt Fest of Jacksonville, 8th
Annual Quilt Show, Jack-
sonville, FL (First Place)

NECTAR COLLECTOR

This is the fourth in a series of painted, whole-cloth quilts. The machine quilting is the major design element in this piece. Top stitching threads in many different colors were used, so that the stitching could be clearly seen against the painted background. Most of the imagery in the quilting came directly out of my imagination. When I was a child I used to lie in the back yard in the summer and watch the clouds. After a while, I could begin to see animals, or faces, or other pictures in the clouds. The quilted images developed in much the same way. I sat and looked at the painted fabric until a picture developed in my mind. Then I quilted the picture. Most of the imagery is of various flowers, leaves, and weeds. These images represent my feelings when I experience flowers and weeds, and not any specific botanical species.

When the quilting was about three-quarters finished, a friend saw the quilt in my studio and said, "You ought to hide a bird in it somewhere." At first I rejected this idea. However, the next morning the large red-orange weed in the center began to look very much like the sort of plant a hummingbird would like, so I quilted in a hummingbird drawing nectar from this plant. Thus the title, "Nectar Collector."

The back of the quilt is black fabric with a side border of commercially-painted fabric. The bobbin threads in the machine quilting are close to the colors of the top threads, and show up clearly against the solid back.

Cleared for Take-Off
56" x 81", 1994

"Cleared for Take-Off," back

CLEARED FOR TAKE-OFF

This is the sixth in a series of painted, whole-cloth quilts, and also part of a series about flights of imagination. The bird image in the quilting was inspired by the great blue herons that nest in a small marsh area a short walk from our farm in northern Illinois. The remainder of the images in the quilting came directly out of my imagination, and were quilted freehand, with no marking of the quilt top.

The back of the quilt is black fabric with a side border of dye-painted fabric. The machine quilting shows up clearly against the black, and creates a night time version of the scene on the front.

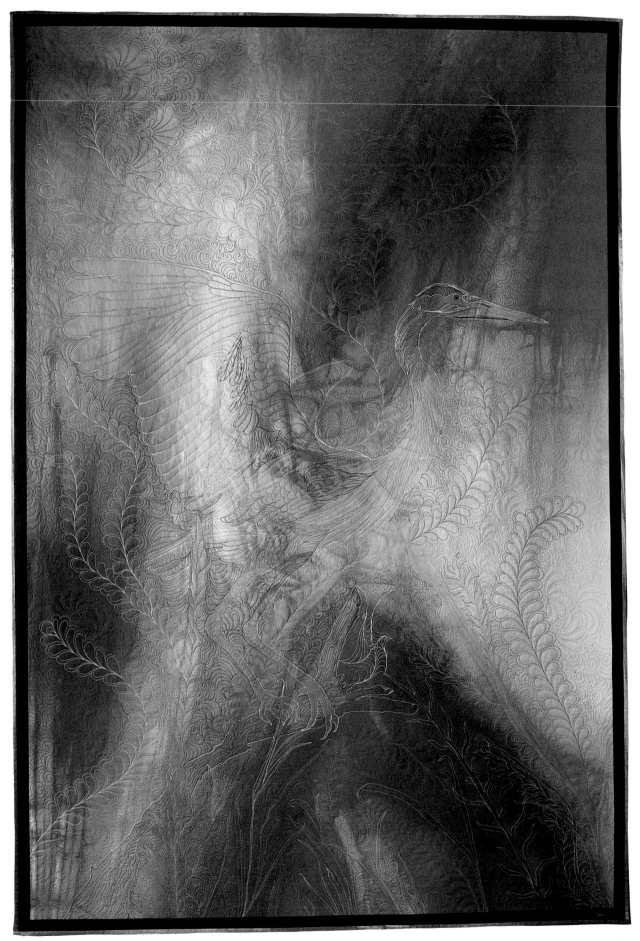

Messenger #1
36½" x 42", 1995
Private Collection

AWARDS

Northeast Quilts Unlimited, Old
Forge Arts Center, 1995, Old
Forge, NY (First Place)

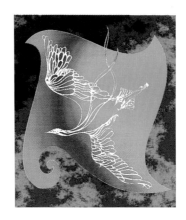

MESSENGER #1

This is one of a series of quilts about birds of the imagination. During the first week of January 1995, my 87-year-old mother had a stroke, which left her a prisoner in her own body, paralyzed and unable to speak, read, or write, but fully conscious of what was happening to her. Driving back and forth to visit her in the hospital, I noticed large white gulls, often solitary, circling in the sky. I have no idea what gulls were doing in the corn fields of Illinois in the middle of winter, but I found comfort in seeing them. I made this small quilt in response to this experience.

Both the center panel fabric and the outer border fabric were painted with fiber reactive dyes. The quilting was done with #30 cotton top stitching thread, which shows up clearly against the background. The bird is surrounded by organic patterns of free machine quilting, done with no additional marking. After quilting, the bird was colored with white prismacolor pencil.

The bird was drawn by hand and scanned into the computer. It was traced using a program called Streamline®, which converted it to a drawing, which could be manipulated in Corel Draw!®. The shape of the center panel, with its curved and spiraled edges, was drawn directly on the screen using bezier curves. The shapes of the center panel and outer border were filled with texture fills altered so that they looked like my hand-painted fabrics. To suggest quilting lines, the shapes of the bird were left unfilled, and the outlines of the shapes were colored white.

The outline of the center panel was printed onto clear acetate, and projected onto hand-painted fabric. After the line was drawn onto the fabric, it was cut out and appliquéd to a darker, hand-painted background fabric. The outline of the bird was projected onto the center panel and traced with a white pencil, for the machine quilting.

Pond at Dusk
44" x 43½", 1995

POND AT DUSK

This is one of a series of whole-cloth quilts created by painting fabric with fiber reactive dye, then quilting the design to give it definition and relief. The design of this fabric painting reminded me of evening at the pond on our farm in Missouri, with the setting sun reflecting on the water. The fabric was quilted heavily by machine in a free-form pattern with no marking of the quilt top. Most of the quilting was done with #30 cotton top-stitching thread. However, in several areas flourescent polyester thread was used to accentuate the reflective quality of the water. Machine quilting is a major design element in this piece, providing a foreground dimension that echoes the patterns of the liquid dyes as they flow together on the cloth.

FIBONACCI'S GARDEN

To me, a garden represents a quiet place where the spirit can rest. In "Fibonacci's Garden" a profusion of lush and vibrant life was created by painting manipulated cotton fabric with fiber reactive dyes. The lattice is pieced from two fabrics. One is striated, and painted in a progression of autumn hues. The other was manipulated into spirals, and painted with vibrant colors to create the illusion of floral and leaf forms. The two fabrics were cut into strips and pieced in the orderly progressions observed in nature by thirteenth-century mathematician Leonardo Fibonacci. A series of circles represent the centering of the mind and spirit that occurs in the garden. The circles are graduated in both size and color, and arc across the surface of the lattice in a diagonal compound curve.

The machine quilting was done with top stitching thread which shows up clearly against the background. It forms patterns of organic leaves, flowers, and the spirals of unfolding life, over the orderly geometry of the pieced design. On the back of the quilt is a fabric painted in clear colorwashes. Against this uncluttered background, the quilted design shows clearly.

Migration #2
88" x 88", 1995
Collection of:
Museum of the American
Quilter's Society, Paducah, KY

AWARDS

Mid-Atlantic Quilt Festival,
1995, Williamsburg, PA (First
Place)

American Quilter's Society
Show, 1995, Paducah, KY
(Best of Show)

MIGRATION #2

"Migration #2" is about what I imagine it would feel like to fly with a flock of migrating birds. Since they are birds of the imagination, they don't represent any particular species. Standing in my garden on my farm in northern Illinois, I can see vast expanses of sky, and almost every day there are flocks of birds passing overhead, migrating, or just traveling together from one pond to the next.

The center fabric was painted with fiber reactive dye in an expressionistic design, incorporating the pure colors of light. The outer border fabric was painted in the greens, browns, and lavenders of earth. A third painted fabric in striated rainbow hues was used to make the center triangles in a variation on the traditional Flying Geese pattern. The silhouettes of 21 machine appliquéd birds fly diagonally from the lower right corner to the upper left corner.

Top stitching thread in many different colors was used for the freehand, free-motion quilting. Long multicolored feathered plumes intertwine the arcs of Flying Geese. In each of the triangles of the Flying Geese the outline of a flying bird is quilted. The center, painted fabric is quilted in patterns of sky and wind. The outer border is quilted in darker, more organic patterns of earth and garden. With the exception of the bird outlines, all of the machine quilting was done freehand, with no marking.

On the back of the quilt is another original variation on Flying Geese. The bobbin threads in the machine quilting echo the colors of the top threads, and mirror the flying bird design on the front of the quilt. The Flying Geese on the back are made from the same striated fabric as those on the front. Another version of this fabric was used to bind the quilt.

"Migration #2," back

AWARDS

From Patches to Neon,
Pennsylvania National Quilt
Extravaganza II, 1995, Fort
Washington, PA (Second
Place)

American International Quilt
Association Show, 1995,
Houston, TX (Honorable Men-
tion & Judges Choice)

DANCING WITH THE SHADOW #1: HARMONY

This is one of a series of quilts about dance. To me, dance symbolizes the energy of life and a sense of creative freedom. The shadow represents the unconscious, from which are drawn visual images of our past experience to create new images in visual art. Although the silhouettes were taken from real dancers, this piece is not so much about the dance itself as about the harmony and beauty that can emerge when we combine our positive energies in creative ways. Each dancer appears to be translucent, and the areas where they overlap become secondary shapes.

The silhouettes of the dancers were scanned into the computer. I used a computer assisted drawing program to manipulate, arrange, and color them to arrive at the final design. The shadow echoes the shapes of the dancers. The composition was printed onto clear acetate, and projected on a sheet of paper-backed fusible web. The silhouette of each dancer and each shadow was drawn, cut from the paper, and fused to hand-painted cotton fabric. Each piece was carefully cut out with embroidery scissors and fused to a background of darker dye-painted fabric.

The fabrics used for the background and the dancers were manipulated while wet. Liquid dyes were poured over them and allowed to flow together in a technique similar to watercolor painting. The shadow was cut from solid black fabric.

A strong border seemed to be needed to contain the energy of the dancers. The border design began with a traditional Crown of Thorns block. This was manipulated on the computer screen in many different ways until I found the combination that best complemented the dancers. The individual blocks were printed out on a laser printer to form templates for the individual pieces.

The geometric outline quilting of the outer border is offset by free-form, free-motion quilting of the center in designs that roughly echo the patterns of the liquid dye as it flowed together in the painting of the dancers and the background fabric.

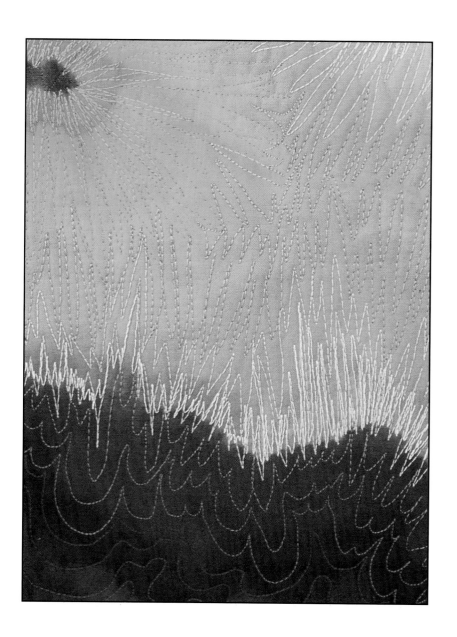

INNER SPACES #1

This is one of a series of quilts exploring spontaneous designs created by painting fabric with fiber-reactive dye, then embroidering and quilting the design to give it definition and relief. The design of this fabric painting reminded me of photographs of various organic substances taken through a microscope. The fabric was heavily quilted by machine in a free-form pattern with no marking of the quilt top. The machine quilting becomes a major design element in this piece, providing a foreground dimension that echoes the painted design.

SEEING THE FOREST FOR THE TREES

This is part of a series of small works in which my process is very much like doodling with fabric. This design was developed spontaneously, working directly on a background with bits of fabric and thread. Each part of the design grew out of the last, just as a doodle grows to fill a page while the mind is engaged elsewhere.

The background fabric was hand painted with fiber-reactive dye. Small scraps of hand-dyed fabric were laid on the painted background and covered with nylon tulle. The figure and trees were appliquéd on top, and the remainder of the design was developed by drawing freehand with my sewing machine and various colors of thread to create an organic composition that is more a landscape of the imagination than a real forest scene.

KIRLIAN FIELDS

The title, "Kirlian Fields," refers to a type of photography which is able to record the fields of electromagnetic energy which surround us in various configurations and colors.

This is the third in a series of small embroidered quilts in which a female figure, cut from hand-painted fabric, is used as part of a dreamlike composition, created with a process very much like doodling with fabric and thread.

The background fabric was hand painted with fiber reactive dye. The figure had already been cut from a second hand-painted fabric, and the leftover scraps were laid on the painted background, leaving the negative outline of the figure. The composition was then stitched with radiating bands of machine embroidery in various colors of thread.

The embroidered composition was surrounded with a border of black fabric and quilted in a free-form design that echoes the embroidered design.

Caryl Bryer Fallert

ABOUT THE AUTHOR

Born in 1947 in Elgin, Illinois, Caryl Bryer Fallert graduated with a BA from Wheaton College in 1969. She also studied art at Illinois State University, University of Wisconsin, and College of DuPage.

During the past ten years, Caryl has gained international recognition for her award-winning art quilts. Her quilts are easily recognized by their scintillating colors and multilevel illusions of light and motion, and she is best known for her three-dimensional "High Tech Tucks" quilts and for her innovative string pieced quilts. Recent works include a series of dye-painted whole cloth quilts.

Caryl's quilts have been exhibited and published extensively, both nationally and internationally. Her work can be found in public and private collections in twenty-two states and six foriegn countries.

Caryl travels frequently, and has lectured and conducted workshops for quilt and textile arts groups throughout the United States, as well as in Japan, Switzerland, Germany, New Zealand, Australia, Ireland, and the People's Republic of China. In 1993, Caryl built her present studio on her farm in Northern Illinois, where she resides with her husband Bob, two horses, five dogs, and a cat.

Caryl can be contacted at PO Box 945, Oswego, Illinois 60543.

COLLECTIONS

MUSEUM
Illinois State Museum, Springfield, IL
Museum of the American Quilter's Society, Paducah, KY

PUBLIC
Wilmette Public Library, Wilmette, IL
Glendale Public Services Building, Glendale, IL
Central Missouri State University, Warrensburg, MO

CORPORATE
Bernina of America, Aurora, IL
Deluxe Check Printers, Lenexa, KS
Fairfield Processing Corp., Danbury, CT
Fidelity Investments, Covington, KY
Fritz Gegauf A. G., Steckborn, Switzerland
General Railway Signal Corp., Rochester, NY
Mark Twain Bancshares Corp., St. Louis, MO
R. R. Street & Co., Inc., Naperville, IL
Sprint Services, Nashville, TN

PRIVATE
Hillary & Marvin Fletcher, USA
Robert & Ardis James, USA
Ray & Susan Scott, USA
Mrs. Yukiko Nakao, Japan
Yuko Watanabe, Japan

Numerous other private collections

SPECIAL AWARDS

1991
Illinois Quilters Hall of Fame
Land of Lincoln Quilt Association

1986
Masterpiece Quilt Award
National Quilting Association

SOLO EXHIBITIONS

1993
College of Du Page, Glen Ellyn, IL
Synnott Associates, Chicago, IL

1992
Ginza Quilt-Eye Gallery, Tokyo, Japan
College of Du Page, Glen Ellyn, IL

1988
American Gallery of Quilts and Textiles, Gig Harbor, WA

1986
The Monroe Gallery, Chicago, IL
Quilting by the Lake Symposium, Cazenovia, NY

1985
American Gallery of Quilts and Textiles, Gig Harbor, WA

SMALL GROUP EXHIBITIONS

1994
Contemporary Quilts: Four Visions in Fiber, Stocker Center Gallery, Elyria, OH

1993
Barrington Area Arts Council Gallery, Barrington, IL

1991
Barrington Area Arts Council Gallery, Barrington, IL

1989
Viewpoints: Textile Arts Center, Chicago, IL

1987
Illini Union Art Gallery: University of Illinois, Urbana, IL

1986
Quilt Invitational: Textile Arts Center, Chicago, IL

SELECTED EXHIBITIONS AND AWARDS

1995

Greater Midwest International, Central Missouri State University, Warrensburg, MO, Juror's Award & Presidents Purchase Award

American Quilter's Society Show & Contest, Paducah, KY, Best of Show

Mid-Atlantic Quilt Festival, Hilton National Conference Center, Williamsburg, PA, First Place

15th Annual Smoky Mountain Quilt Show, Dogwood Arts Festival, Knoxville, TN, Best Wall Quilt & Best Machine Techniques

1995 Crabby Award — For Excellence in the Visual Arts, *Art Calendar Magazine*

Quilt America, Indianapolis Convention Center, Indianapolis, IN, Third Place & Honorable Mention

Quilters Unlimited Showcase, Blue Springs, MO, Third Place

Dallas Quilt Celebration, Market Hall, Dallas, TX, Honorable Mention

Columbus Heritage Quilt Show, Columbus, IN, Third Place

Fantastic Fibers 1995, Yeiser Arts Center, Paducah, KY

Creative and Innovative Quilts, Rocky Mountain Quilt Museum, Golden, CO

22nd Anniversary National Juried Exhibit, Wisconsin Women in the Arts, Anderson Art Center, Kenosha, WI

Log Cabin Quilts: New Quilts from Old Favorites, Museum of the American Quilter's Society, Paducah, KY, and traveling, March 1995 – January 1997

Clay, Fiber, Paper, Wood, Metal, Glass, Octagon Center for the Arts, Ames, IA

Buds, Blades, and Bowers, Aullwood Audubon Center, Dayton, OH, Craftsmanship Award

A World of Quilts XVI, Northern Star Quilters Invitational, Somers, NY

The Essential Textile, Guilford Handcrafts Center, Guilford, CT

Full Deck Art Quilts, Renwick Gallery, The Smithsonian, Washington, DC, and traveling

Studio Art Quilt Associates Show, Museum of the American Quilter's Society, Paducah, KY

Studio Art Quilt Associates Show, Dollywood, Pigeon Forge, TN

Invitational Exhibition of Contemporary Quilts, Round Top Center for the Arts, Damariscotta, ME

Patchwork Pride, Quilters Heritage Celebration, Lancaster, PA

Recursos de Santa Fe, Santa Fe Quilt Festival — Invitational, Santa Fe, NM

Small Works, The Gallery at Studio B, Lancaster, OH

Here to There, New York Quilt Festival Invitational Show, New York, NY

Natural Impression, Santa Barbara Museum of Natural History, Santa Barbara, CA

Bold New Quilts and Tomorrow's Treasures, New York Quilt Festival, New York, NY

Threads, GCA, Mountaintop Gallery, Catskill, NY

A Celebration of Creativity, Crossman Gallery, Whitewater, WI

American Quilters Showcase, four locations in England

From Patches to Neon, Pennsylvania National Quilt Extravaganza II, Fort Washington, PA

Materials: Hard and Soft, Meadows Gallery, The Art Center, Denton, TX

Quiltfest of Jacksonville, Jacksonville, FL, Best of Show, Second Place, Best Machine Quilting, First Place

The Textile Medium III, The Arts Chateau, Butte, MT

Capitol Quilt Festival Invitational, Frankfort, KY

Quilts=Art=Quilts, Schweinfurth, Auburn, NY, First Place, Judges Choice

Greater Midwest International Invitational, Central Missouri State University, Warrensburg, MO

Quilting in the Tetons, Jackson, WY, First Place — Whole Cloth

American International Quilt Association Show, Houston, TX, First Place, Honorable Mention, Judges Choice

Shapes and Patterns, Eastcoast Quilters Alliance, Westford, MA, Honorable Mention, Second Place

Facet Invitational Exhibition, De Kalb County Quilters Show, De Kalb, IL

Northeast Quilters Unlimited, Old Forge Arts Center, Old Forge, NY, First Place

United Nations Fiftieth Anniversary Friendship Quilts, USA Block Contest, New York Quilt Festival, First Place

1994

Mid-Atlantic Quilt Festival V, Williamsburg, VA

American Quilter's Society Show & Contest, Paducah, KY

Capitol Quilt Festival, Invitational Exhibition, Frankfort, KY

Fifth Annual National Quilt Exhibition, Hill Country Arts Foundation, Ingram, TX, Second Place

Interrelationships Naturally: Fabric in Flight, Aullwood Audubon Center, Dayton, OH

Celebration of Excellence (Invitational for former AQS Best of Show winners and new work), Museum of the American Quilter's Society, Paducah, KY

The Artist as Quiltmaker VI, Fava Gallery, Oberlin, OH

Chautauqua International for Fiber Art, Chautauqua Craft Alliance, Adams Art Gallery, Dunkirk, NY

Spectrum — An Array of Art Quilts, Quilt Capers Gallery, Oldwick, NJ

Small Works, The Gallery at Studio B, Lancaster, OH

Secret Gardens: Traditional and Contemporary Quilts by American Quiltmakers, Thomas Center Gallery, Gainsville, FL, Distinguished Artist Award

Crafts National 28, Zoller Gallery, University Park, PA

Best of Show Quilts, National Quilting Association Silver Jubilee Celebration, Charleston, WV

22nd Annual National Quilt Competition, Western Heritage Center, Billings, MT, Viewers Choice, First Place & Best Use of Color

Northern Lights, Contemporary Fiber Exhibit, Convergence 94, Minneapolis, MN

West Coast Quilters Conference: Computer Quilt Show, Sacramento, CA

Quilts Now, Invitational Contemporary Art Quilt Exhibit, Oklahoma City Art Museum, Oklahoma City, OK

Quilt Art — A Contemporary View, Textilmuseum Max Berk, Heidelberg, Germany

Colors of Earth and Space, NASA Ames Research Center, Visitors' Center, Moffett Field, CA

Into the Future — AIQA Members Quilts, Invitational Exhibit, European Quilt Market, Karlsruhe, Germany and Spring Quilt Market, St. Louis, MO

Textile Arts Center: Members' Show, Chicago, IL

Quilt America, Kokomo, IN

Art Quilt International '94, Penny Nii Quilt Art Gallery, Mountain View, CA

Art Quilt International: Japan, Tokyo, Japan

Colors and Visual Perceptions, Quiltfest USA, Louisville, KY

From Sea to Shining Sea, Pennsylvania National Quilt Extravaganza, Philadelphia, PA, Honorable Mention

Quiltfest USA: Invitational Exhibit, Louisville, KY

Intuition: The Direction in Craft, Gallery of Artifacts and Treasures, Daytona Beach, FL

Harvest of Time IV Quilt Show, McHenry County College, Crystal Lake, IL

My Best Quilt, Kokusai Art, Shinjuku Mitsudoshi Department Store, Tokyo, Japan

Pacific International Quilt Festival, San Francisco, CA, Honorable Mention

1994 Fiber Competition and Exhibition, Sponsored by BASF, Creative Arts Guild, Dalton, GA

Quilt Fest of Jacksonville, 8th Annual Quilt Show, Jacksonville, FL, First Place

Childhood Images and Dreams, Chatfield College, St. Martin, OH

Merced Courthouse Museum, Penny Nii Gallery, Merced, CA

From Patchworks to Artworks, Rocklin, CA

Mountain Treasures, The Armory, Hendersonville, NC, First Place

Hill Country Arts Foundation, Sixth Annual National Juried Quilt Exhibition, Ingram, TX

Quilts=Art=Quilts, Schweinfurth Memorial Arts Center, Auburn, NY, Judges Choice

Speaking of Values, Eastcoast Quilters Alliance, Westford, MA, First Place — Quilting excellence and First Place — Craftsmanship

American International Quilt Association Show, Houston, TX, First Place and Award of Merit

1993

Fourth Annual National Quilt Exhibition, Hill Country Arts Foundation, Ingram, TX, Third Place

Mid-States Craft Exhibition, Evansville Museum of Art, Evansville, IN

Paper/Fiber, Johnson County Arts Council, Iowa City, IA

Quilt Crazy, Exhibition of Contemporary Quilts, The Lobby Gallery, New York, NY

Clay & Fiber, Octagon Center for the Arts, Ames, IA

Fantastic Fibers, Yeiser Art Center, Paducah, KY

Mid-Atlantic Quilt Festival, Williamsburg, PA, Second Place

Contemporary American Quilts, Crafts Council Gallery, London, England, Crafts Council of Ireland, Dublin; Shipley Art Gallery, Gateshead, England

Art That Pushes the Limits, Surya Art Gallery, Lincoln, NE

The Textile Medium: Contemporary Expression in Quiltmaking, Arts Chateau, Butte, MT, First Place

Interrelationships Naturally, Aullwood Audubon Center, Dayton, OH, Best of Show, Craftsmanship Award & People's Choice

Chautauqua International for Fiber Art, Adams Art Gallery, Dunkirk, NY

New Textiles, Mobilia Gallery, Cambridge, MA

Mid-Atlantic Quilt Festival, Williamsburg, VA, Second Place

Quilt America, Indianapolis Convention Center, Indianapolis, IN, Third Place

Quilt Connection All Stars, Great American Quilt Festival, Museum of American Folk Art, New York, NY, Honorable Mention

Crafts National, Zoller Gallery, University Park, PA

New Wave Quilt: International Quiltmaking as an Art Form, Brea Cultural Center Gallery, Brea, CA

Quilters Unlimited, 1st Annual Mid-America Quilters Showcase, Kansas City, MO, Honorable Mention

American Quilter's Society Show, Paducah, KY, First Place & Third Place

A Celebration of Creativity, Crossman Gallery, Whitewater, WI, Award of Merit

Fiber Celebrated '93, Nevada State Museum, Las Vegas, NV

"Protecting and Replenishing Our Earth's Resources," Chesapeake Quilt Festival, Towsan, MD, Second Place

Art Quilt International '93, Leone-Nii Gallery, Mountain View, CA

Fiber Arts, The Creative Arts Guild, Dalton, GA

Northeast Quilts Unlimited, Arts Center of Old Forge, Old Forge, NY, Third Place

Quilts=Art=Quilts, Schweinfurth Memorial Art Center, Auburn, NY, First Place

American International Quilt Association. Show, Houston, TX, Award of Merit

1992

Mid-States Craft Exhibition, Evansville Museum of Arts and Science, Evansville, IN

Currents '92, Barn Art Gallery, MTSU, Murfreesboro, TN

The Artist as Quiltmaker, Fireland Association. for the Visual Arts, Oberlin, OH

Quilts as a New Art Form II, Janis Wetsman Collection, Birmingham, MI

New Wave Quilt Collection International Artists Series, Quilt Art of Japan, traveling throughout Japan

Quilts: Discovering a New World, Quilt Expo, Europa III, Netherlands

Quilts Now: The Kentucky Quilt Project, Zephyr Gallery, Louisville, KY

Pattern Pattern Pattern, Mesa Arts Center, Mesa, AZ

National Art Competition, Northeast Missouri State University, Kirksville, MO

National Exhibition of Depth and Diversity in Contemporary American Art, Museum Without Walls International, Bemus Point, NY

Celebrating the Stitch, Newton Arts Center, Newtonville, MA, three year traveling exhibit

42nd Annual Quad-State Exhibition, Quincy Art Center, Quincy, IL

Visions: The Art of the Quilt, Museum of San Diego History, San Diego, CA

Paper/Fiber, Johnson County Arts Council, Iowa City, IA, Third Place

Fantastic Fibers, Yeiser Art Center, Paducah, KY

Needle Expressions, Nelson Fine Arts Center, Tempe, AZ

Crafts National, Zoller Gallery, State College, PA

Fabric '92, Quilt/Surface Design Symposium, Columbus, OH, Fourth Place

A Celebration of Creativity, Fiber & Textile Exhibit, Crossman Gallery, Whitewater, WI, Award of Merit & Honorable Mention

Art Flourishes, Barrington Area Arts Council Gallery, Barrington, IL

Materials: Hard and Soft, Greater Denton Arts Council, Denton, TX

Patterns International, Northern Kentucky University Art Gallery, Highland Heights, KY

Quilts: Contemporary Voices from the Plains, Gallery 181, Iowa State University, Ames, IA

Quilts=Art=Quilts, Schweinfurth Art Center, Auburn, NY

Autumn Gathering, Anderson Arts Center, Kenosha, WI

Color Light and Motion, The Works Gallery, Philadelphia, PA

1991

Quilt National '91, The Dairy Barn Arts Center, Athens, OH

Art and Music / Music and Art, Contemporary Art Workshop, Chicago, IL

41st Quad State Art Exhibition, Quincy Art Center, Quincy, IL

Two & Three Dimensional Art Competition, Lafayette Art Association, Lafayette, LA

Quilts as a New Art Form, The Janis Wetsman Collection, Birmingham, MI

National Quilting Association 22nd Annual Quilt Show, Lincoln, NE, First Place

Fiber Celebrated '91, Intermountain Weavers Conference, Colorado Springs, CO, First Place

Contemporary Art Workshop: Summer Invitational Exhibit, Chicago, IL

Annual Quilt Exhibition, Western Heritage Center, Billings, MT, First Place

Quilts=Art=Quilts, Schweinfurth Memorial Art Center, Auburn, NY

A Celebration of Creativity, Crossman Gallery, Whitewater, WI, Certificate of Merit

Aesthetics '91, Friendship Hall Gallery, McPherson, KS

The Textile Medium: Contemporary Expressions in Quiltmaking, Arts Chateau, Butte, MT, Best of Show

New Art Forms: 20th Century Decorative and Applied Arts Chicago International, Navy Pier, Chicago, IL

American International Quilt Association Show, Houston, TX, Juror's Choice & First Place (2 categories)

"Piles of Pile" Unconventional Pile by Contemporary Artists, Textile Arts International, Minneapolis, MN

The Chicago Connection: Contemporary Works in Fiber, Hinsdale Center for the Arts, Hinsdale, IL

Surface Design, Rochester Art Center, Winona State University, Rochester, MN

New Wave Quilt Collection, Quilt Art of Japan, traveling throughout Japan

Botanics, Gallery Ten, Rockford, IL

1990

The Definitive Contemporary American Quilt, Bernice Steinbaum Gallery, New York, NY, three year traveling exhibition

Innovative Traditions, The Museums of Stony Brook, Stony Brook, NY

40th Illinoiain Juried Art Show, Quincy Art Center, Quincy, IL, Second Place

Aesthetics '90, Friendship Hall Gallery, McPherson, KS

Fiber as Art, Hunterdon Art Center, Clinton, NJ, Honorable Mention

Needle Expressions: Council of American Embroiderers, two year traveling exhibit

The Quilt Movement, Dairy Barn Art Center, Athens, OH, Best of Show

Fabric Gardens Traveling Exhibit, Japan, 1990, USA, 1991–92

American International Quilt Association Show, Houston, TX, First Place

1989

Fiber Celebrated, Salt Lake City Art Center, Salt Lake City, UT, Best of Show

American Quilter's Society Show, Paducah, KY, First Place (wall quilt) & Best of Show

Breaking New Ground, New England Quilt Museum, Lowell, MA

American International Quilt Association Show, Houston, TX, First Place

Hill Country Arts Foundation: First Annual Quilt Show, Ingram, TX, Best of Show

Fiber National, Adams Art Gallery, Dunkirk, NY

Quilts=Art=Quilts, Schweinfurth Memorial Art Center, Auburn, NY, Jurors Choice

1988

Needle Expressions, Council of American Embroiderers, two year traveling show

Quilts Not To Sleep With, Wilson Art Center, Rochester, NY

American Quilter's Society Show, Paducah, KY, First Place

The Intimate Eye, Chicago Womens Caucus for Art, Artemesia Gallery, Chicago, IL

Quilts=Art=Quilts, Schweinfurth Memorial Art Center, Auburn, NY, Jurors Choice

Cross Current: Art to Wear, Northern Illinois University Gallery, Chicago, IL

1987

Fiber National, Adams Art Gallery, Dunkirk, NY

Stitchery '87 International, Pittsburgh, PA

Quilt National '87, Dairy Barn Art Center, Athens, OH, three year traveling exhibit

Contemporary Quilts, Boston University Art Gallery and U. S. Information Service, three year exhibit, traveled throughout Europe

Art to Wear V, Colorado Gallery of the Arts, Littleton, CO, Best of Show

1986

The View from Above, Smithsonian Institution, Air and Space Museum, Washington, DC

New Dimensions in Fiber II, College of DuPage Art Gallery, Wheaton, IL, Jurors' Choice

1985

National Quilting Association Show, Sanford, FL, Best of Show

Stitchery '85 International, Pittsburgh, PA

Art to Wear III, Colorado Gallery of the Arts, Littleton, CO, Best of Show

American Quilter's Society Show, Paducah, KY, First Place

SELECTED PUBLICATIONS

MAGAZINES

American Magazines

American Craft, Dec 90/Jan 91, p. 84

Americana, Aug 91, pp. 35–36

A.I.Q.A. Quarterly
1990: Vol X #1, pp. 8, 13
1991: Spring, p. 15, Fall p. 2
1994: Winter, p. 6
1995: Spring, p. 17

American Quilter
1985: Fall, p. 28, Winter, p. 5
1987: Spring, pp. 14–16
(cover & feature)/ Fall, p. 49
1988: Fall, p. 25
1989: Fall, pp. 38, 41, 48, 49
(both covers)
1990: Fall, pp. 2, 14–21, 41, 45 (feature)
1993: Fall, pp. 44 & 48
1994: Summer, p. 35
1995: Summer, p. 32
Fall, pp. 3, 28, 29
(front and back cover)

Art Quilt Magazine
1994: Premiere Issue, pp. 10 & 35
1995: Issue #3, pp. 23 & 40

Chicago Tribune: Sunday Tempo
1990: June 17, pp. 1, 6 (feature)

Creative Ideas For Living
1988: Sept/Oct, pp. 32, 33, 120–125
(feature)

Fiberarts
1991: Summer, p. 48
1992: Nov/Dec, p. 56
1995: Mar/Apr, pp. 53 & 60

The Flying Needle
1989: Feb pp. 3–6 (cover and feature)
1991: Feb p. 15

Lady's Circle Patchwork Quilts
1991: July/Aug, pp. 20, 22
1994: May, pp. 21, 23

Miniworks
1993: Spring, p. 40

Patchwork Patter
1985: Nov, pp. 20–21 (cover and feature)
1986: Nov, p. 7
1991: Feb, p. 10 (cover and feature)

Quilt
1984: Winter, p. 13

Quilters Newsletter Magazine
1984: Jan, p. 21
1986: Feb, p. 4
Nov/Dec , p. 6
1987: Feb, p. 36
May, p. 6
Sept, pp. 23–27 (feature)
1988: Jan, p. 29
Feb, p. 15
July/Aug, pp. 24–25 (feature)
1989: Feb, p. 10
1990: Jan, p. 6
Feb, p. 38
July/Aug, p. 6
1991: Jan/Feb, p. 10
May, p. 6
June, pp. 6, 7
Dec, p. 8
1992: Jan/Feb, pp. 32–33 (feature)
March, p. 2 (cover)
May, p. 8
1993: June, p. 12
Sept, p. 23
1994: Sept, p. 22
Dec, p. 9
1995: March, pp. 40–41
July/Aug, p. 8

Quilting International
1990: Sept, pp. 16–17
Nov, pp. 46–47
1993: Nov, p. 28–29
1994: Vol #34, March, p. 48
May, p. 18
Sept, cover & p. 2
1995: May, p. 38

Quilting Today
1991: Apr/May, p. 62
1992: Apr, pp. 3,10

Quilt Show
1989: Issue #2, pp. 25, 30, 31
Issue #4, p. 21

Quilt World
1987: Apr, p. 33
Summer, p. 39
1988: May, p. 31
1990: Feb/Mar, p. 33

San Diego Home and Garden
1990: May, p. 132

Stardate (Astronomy Magazine)
1990: May/Jun, p. 17

Surface Design Journal
1991: Summer, p. 27
1992: Summer p. 29
1995: Vol 19 #2, Winter, p. 25

Australian Magazines

Craft Arts
1992: Issue #25, p. 115

Russian Magazines

Rukodilie (Magazine of the Needle Arts)
1995: p. 29

German Magazines

Patchwork Gilde
1994: Heft 35, p. 12
1995: Heft 39, p. 30

Japanese Magazines

My Patchwork Quilt In The World
1991: Vol, #1, p. 115

Patchwork Quilt Senka
1991: Summer, p. 77
1995: Autumn, p. 78

Patchwork Quilt Tsushin
1987: Issue #22, p. 104
1989: Issue #33, p. 17
1992: Issue #48 (cover and feature), pp. 20–25

Quilt Japan
1988: Vol #11
1990: Vol #14, pp. 82–83 (feature)

New Zealand Magazines

North and South
1992: July, p. 21

The Arts Advocate
1993: Apr, p. 12

Listener
1993: May 1–6, p. 9

Contact
1993: May 13, p. 9

New Zealand Quilter
1993: July, p. 10

BOOKS AND CATALOGS
English Language

American Quilts
1991: Publications International, pp. 58–61

Art Quilts: Playing with a Full Deck
1985: Pierce & Suit – Pomegranate, pp. 76–77

Attic Windows: A Contemporary View
1988: Leone Publishing Co., p. 38

Award Winning Quilts and Their Makers
1991: Vol 1, AQS, p. 36
1992: Vol II, AQS, pp. 30, 31, 92, 93, 156, 157
1993: Vol III, AQS, pp. 76–77
1994: Vol IV, AQS, pp. 140–141 & 170–171

Back Art: On the Flip Side
1991: Rafalovich & Pellman, Leone Publishing Co., pp. 32, 33, 58, 59

Celebrating the Stitch
1991: Barbara Lee Smith, Taunton Press, p. 45

The Complete Book of Machine Quilting
1994: Robbie & Tony Fanning, Chilton, p. 2

Contemporary American Quilts
1993: Crafts Council, London, England, pp. 24, 25, 51

Contemporary Quilts from Traditional Designs
1988: Mosey, E. P. Dutton Press, p. 15

Contemporary Quilts, U.S.A.
1990: U. S. Information Agency (international distribution only), p. 46

Creative American Quilting
1989: Better Homes and Gardens, p. 248

The Definitive Contemporary American Quilt
1990: Bernice Steinbaum, p. 30

88 Leaders in the Quilt World Today
Nihon Vogue Publishing Co., Tokyo, Japan, pp. 12–13

Excellence of Excellencies:
New Wave Quilts 1
1990: pp. 74–80

New Wave Quilts II
1992: pp. 26, 27, 83
Setsuko Segawa, Mitsumura Suiko Shoin

Fabric Gardens
1990: Asahi Shimbun, p. 56

Fiberarts Design Book 4
1991: Lark Books, p. 95

Fiber Expressions, The Contemporary Quilt
1987: Schiffer Pub., p. 49 (cover)

Fourteen Easy Baby Quilts
1990: Dittman, p. 57

Innovative Traditions:
New Expressions in Contemporary Quiltmaking
1990: The Museums at Stony Brook
Machine Quilting Made Easy
1994: Maurine Nobel, That Patchwork Place, p. 29

The Magical Effects of Color
1992: Joen Wolfrom, C&T Publishing, pp. 62, 63, 68

Mother Plays with Dolls
1990: Bailey, pp. 70–71

Needle Expressions (catalog)
1988: Council of American Embroiderers, p. 2
1990: p. 1

The New Quilt 1: Dairy Barn Quilt National
1991: Taunton press, p. 41

Perfect Pineapples
1989: Hall & Haywood, C&T Publishing, p. 38

Plays; Level 1 & Plays; Level II
1989: Jamestown Publishers (cover art)

Precision Pieced Quilts
1992: Haywood & Hall, Chilton, pp. 21, 44, 76, 97, 117

Quilt Art: A Contemporary View
Textilmuseum Max Berk, cover and pp. 19–20

The Quilt Connection All Stars
1993: Museum of American Folk Art, p. 15

Quilt Digest 4
1985: Quilt Digest Press, p. 42

Quilts: Discovering a New World
1992: Leman Publications, p. 25

Quilts: Old & New, A Similar View
1993: AQS, Pilgrim & Roy, p. 27

Quilts: The Permanent Collection –
Museum of the American Quilter's Society
1991: AQS, pp. 19, 67

The Quintessential Quilt
1994: Commemorative Catalogue of the International Quilt Festival, p. 28

Singer Sewing Update #2
1989: p. 55

Successful Machine Quilting
1995: Marti Michell, Meredith Press, p. 156

Superstars: A Decade of Design
1988: Fairfield Processing Corp., p. 16

Visions: Quilts of a New Decade
1990: C&T Publishing, p. 38

Visions: The Art of the Quilt
1992: C&T Publications, pp. 4 & 55

Japanese Language

International Quilt Art Exhibition
1988: pp. 16–17

Shining Star: 1988 from U.S.A.
1988: p. 26

New Wave American Quilt
1991: Exhibit Catalog, pp. 49–52, 77

CALENDARS

Bernina 100 Year Anniversary Calendar: 1993
Fritz Gegauf AG, Apr

The Quilt Calendar, 1993
Yuko Watanabe (Japan) July/Aug

Quilt Art '85, AQS Books
Quilt Art '87, AQS Books
Quilt Art '91, AQS Books

American Quilter's Society Wall Calendar,
AQS Books
1989:
1990: (cover)
1996: (cover)

Quiltmakers: 1988
Leone Publications, June

OTHER PUBLICATIONS

American Quilter's Society show poster, 1990, 1996

Fire Within, 1990: Libana (music group) cover art for cassette, CD, and songbook

High Tech Tucks #33, poster
1992: Yuko Watanabe, Japan

Corona II, jigsaw puzzle
1992: AQS

INDEX

Bold number indicates full quilt.

AQS BOOKS ON QUILTS

This is only a partial listing of the books on quilts that are available from the American Quilter's Society. AQS books are known the world over for their timely topics, clear writing, beautiful color photographs, and accurate illustrations and patterns. Most of the following books are available from your local bookseller, quilt shop, or public library. If you are unable to locate certain titles in your area, you may order by mail from the AMERICAN QUILTER'S SOCIETY, P.O. Box 3290, Paducah, KY 42002-3290. Customers with Visa or MasterCard may phone in orders from 7:00–4:00 CST, Monday–Friday, Toll Free 1-800-626-5420. Add $2.00 for postage for the first book ordered and $0.40 for each additional book. Include item number, title, and price when ordering. Allow 14 to 21 days for delivery.